how
People Who Don't
Know They're Dead
attach themselves to
unsuspecting bystanders
and what to do about it

GARY LEON HILL

WEISERBOOKS
Boston, MA/York Beach, ME

First published in 2005 by
Red Wheel/Weiser, LLC
York Beach, ME
With offices at:
368 Congress Street
Boston, MA 02210
www.redwheelweiser.com

*Cover photo: Wally Johnston, Evelyn Johnston, and Ruth Johnston (center)
at the wedding of the author's parents, 1938.*

Library of Congress Cataloging-in-Publication Data
Hill, Gary Leon.
People who don't know they're dead : how they attach themselves to
unsuspecting bystanders and what to do about it / Gary Leon Hill.
p. cm.
Includes bibliographical references.
ISBN 1-57863-297-8
1. Spirit possession. 2. Johnston, Wally. I. Title.
BF1555.H395 2005
133.9—dc22
2005004150

Typeset in 12 point Minion by Sky Peck Design
PRINTED IN CANADA
TCP
12 11 10 09 08 07 06 05
8 7 6 5 4 3 2 1

The invisible is the source of the visible.
—DR. CARL WICKLAND

Ninety-nine percent of reality is invisible.
—BUCKMINSTER FULLER

The world is made up of stories, not of atoms.
—MURIEL RUKEYSER

Table of Contents

Acknowledgments

FIRST, THANKS TO WALLY, WHOSE STORY THIS IS. The book would not exist without him. His other books—*Take Charge: A Guide to Feeling Good* and *Possible Fatal*, which he wrote with Joanie Thurston—are available through Acorn Endeavors, PO Box 301056, Portland, OR 97230.

Thanks to Ardis. Thanks to Lorraine Darr and Vic and to all those who came through them. To Laurel and Evelyn and Mona for their help. To Patricia Switzer, Moss Kaplan, and David Dower for their feedback. Thanks to Jocelyn and Frank.

Thanks to Red Wheel/Weiser and everybody there. To Michael Kerber, and especially, Jan Johnson, who said yes to the idea and then gave it her support. She is a terrific editor and good friend.

And thanks to Ruth. "Sometimes I think maybe we're crazy," she told me. "But everything I keep learning fits together and I have yet to learn anything that really contradicts what's gone before and that's why I continue with my basic mode of living that 'Farther along, we'll know more about it.'"

Finally, thanks to those I know are with me but I do not see.

Introduction

"EINSTEIN SAID THE MOST IMPORTANT QUESTION a human being can ask is this," Wally Johnston told me. "Is the universe friendly or unfriendly? If you believe the universe is friendly, if that's a basic belief, then you go out and engage the universe. If you believe the universe is unfriendly and out to get your ass, you pull back and you don't get the experience. You don't learn. You're in a protective mode all the time instead of a healing, growing mode.

"So, I think if I were to come into psychology today, I would work in the belief area. And that is one of the beliefs that I would check on in many different ways. Is the universe friendly or unfriendly?

"The other would be Dostoyevsky's vote for the most important question you can ask: What happens at death? As amplified by Dag Hammarskjöld, who said: 'It is our concept of death that decides our answers to all of the questions which life poses.'"

Albert Einstein was a German-born American physicist. Fyodor Dostoyevsky was a Russian novelist. Dag Hammarskjöld was a Swedish diplomat and Secretary General of the United Nations from 1953 to 1961.

Wally Johnston is my uncle.

■   ■   ■

In the vaulted central room of a manufactured home on a side street in northeast Portland, Oregon, five people sit in a circle around the dining room table. Were it daytime, sunlight would be flooding in around them. Lush, leafy green plants would be respirating audibly. It is night.

> **Wally:** *Let's get relaxed and centered. Set aside all of our own concerns. Create a bubble of light from your own heart area. Allow the feeling of love and warmth in the heart to expand and manifest as golden-white light expanding, expanding, until it is a bubble around each of us, and the bubbles touch and create a ring of golden-white light.*
>
> *Now, thinking of the light and the ring of light, if you would repeat after me:*
>
>> *The light of God surrounds us.*
>> *The love of God enfolds us.*
>> *The power of God protects us.*
>> *The presence of God watches over us.*
>> *Wherever we are, God is.*
>
> *Now, through the pendulum, we ask Universal Intelligence for permission to work with the Higher Self of Lyle Hoop.*

Ruth holds a six-inch chain from which a teardrop stone hangs motionless in the air. The stone begins to move with a clock-wise motion. Ruth nods to Wally.

> **Wally**: *We have permission to work with the Higher Self of Lyle Hoop.*
>
> *Now we call into this circle the Higher Self of Lyle Hoop and any entities that may be attached to his body or his aura and energy system. Is the Higher Self of Lyle Hoop present?*

Again, Ruth's pendulum begins to circle in a clockwise direction. She nods.

> **Wally**: *At this point, we'd like to speak to any and all entities, any stowaways or hitchhiking entities who are in the energy system and the aura of Lyle Hoop. And we know that one is there and that it is Lyle's father, Charley. We are speaking to you, Charley Hoop.*
>
> *You are in Lyle Hoop's body, a body which does not belong to you, Charley. Your own body is dead. This may come as a surprise to you, but we've learned that being dead is so much like being alive that many people have died without realizing their condition.*

■ ■ ■

My mother's mother lived in Lincoln, Nebraska, too, so when her sons and daughters and their wives and husbands and my cousins came through town, they'd all wind up around the table at our house to visit. The Johnston clan could visit. I heard a lot of talk.

The ones I paid most attention to, even as a child, were my mother's youngest sister, Ruth, a psychiatric nurse who worked with schizophrenics, and her brother, my parapsychological uncle Wally.

By the end of the sixties, when I'd come back from living in San Francisco, and we sat around that table, Ruth and Wally and I got to nodding back and forth. With twenty and twenty-six years between us, we were finding ourselves on the same wavelength.

Ten years later, Wally and I were helping Ruth move across the country. The plan was that Ruth would take the plants and the cat in her car and Wally and I would trade off driving the rental truck, but mostly I just rode along. Wally liked to drive, mostly without talking.

Until late one afternoon when a dark lid lifted over Iowa and the world lit up. The sky and highway turned chrome and the horizon melted, and handful after handful of illuminated rain like splattering mercury exploded against the windshield.

Calmly, Wally focused on the light beyond the windshield and began to talk about the spirits he had counseled.

When the universe restored itself and things were looking normal, I let some Earth Time pass, then asked if he had happened to tape record any of those sessions.

Just this side of Council Bluffs, he said he had. Two shoeboxes full. Six months later, I had transcribed all of the tapes in both shoeboxes, three hundred single-spaced pages.

Seven years after that, he and Ruth sat in the Denver audience of a play I had written about earthbound spirits who attach themselves to an unsuspecting pair of tape transcribers.

Thirteen years after that, I started writing this book.

The sixties, seventies, eighties, and nineties was an arcing arrow. Things changed fast. Mostly our minds. And how we think about our minds. And matter. And mind *over* matter. And consciousness and energy and auras and holistic health, telepathy and altered states and reincarnation, out-of-body experiences and life after death.

With everything that's been learned in the past forty years, this book could have gone off in many directions. I chose to follow Wally. I start where he did. I reference the books he read and fed to me, and write about the people he became interested in in much the same order he did—Elisabeth Kubler-Ross, Raymond Moody, Elmer Green, Carl Wickland, Bob Monroe.

I've known Wally all my life. When he told me he'd been talking to the spirits of people who were dead and did not know it, I didn't ask him to prove it. I said, "Let me hear those tapes. Here, let me type those up." And I did. And I made copies. Then I followed him through that door.

People Who Don't Know They're Dead is about that pull of time and how Wally, Ruth, and I found ourselves moving through it, what we learned, and how it changed us. The book begins with people who *do* know they are dead because that is where it started.

First Mention of Spirits

"THE FIRST MENTION OF SPIRITS," Wally told me, "was when we were in the SEARCH group who brought in a lot of parapsychology stuff to Rochester. We got acquainted with Brother Joel Nelson who was getting along in years and wasn't able to drive anymore, so we were the natural ones to take him. Brother Joel taught mind control at St. Mary's College in Winona and was kind of a status symbol, so being his driver, we got invited to have lunch with Ram Dass and Susy Smith and all the people who were brought in to speak."

Brother Joel soon told them they should get to know Vic and Lorraine Darr, that Vic was a reflexologist and probably a healer, and that Lorraine had begun to do automatic writing. So, Wally made an appointment for his wife, Ardis, and they drove the fifty-odd miles from their home in Winona, Minnesota to Vic's Rochester office. Ardis's feet were in Vic's lap when Lorraine came down the steps with Brother Joel.

"I later found out they'd been upstairs in the back office talking to spirits," Wally said. But that first day all they knew was that when Lorraine came down the stairs, she said: "How many do you have down here?"

"Well, there's been a young one standing right beside Ardis ever since I started," answered Vic.

"Oh, hi, Mom and Dad," said Lorraine. "I just wanted to let you know I'm still around and it was a very easy death. No pain."

Michael had been born to Ardis and Wally on November 15, 1957. He died seven years, four months and nine days later when he was hit by a car after sliding down a snow bank near his house. He had been dead ten years and now appeared to be speaking through a woman they had yet to be introduced to.

"Oh, it's yours," said Lorraine.

"We weren't really ready to talk," Wally told me. "This was new to us. And so we kind of ignored it."

"I didn't ignore it," said Ardis.

It was hard to ignore. Ten years after Michael's death in Vermillion, South Dakota, three hundred miles east in Rochester, Minnesota, this woman who had no way of knowing they had lost a child or that his death had been an easy one, either now knew both of these things about Michael or had gone somewhere else while his spirit used her body to say hi.

There'd been one car on the street. The sidewalk was high. He'd been sledding with a friend and was hurrying home down the steep snow bank and couldn't stop because of four new inches of powder. The driver slammed on her brakes and slid forty-two feet. If she'd kept sliding straight ahead, she could have come to a halt, backed up an inch, and Michael would have jumped up and walked away, Wally said. As it was, she swerved to miss him, tried to turn into a driveway, lost control of her car, and slammed him into the curb. She went up over the curb and peeled off part of his jacket on the right front chrome fender of her two-tone '64 Pontiac LeMans hardtop. Wally remembers every detail. Michael still had his golashes on at the hospital, he said.

"I was the only one that talked to the guy who called the ambulance and held him until they came. It was the coroner's report that said his spleen had ruptured, that he'd bled internally, just faded away."

"It was a very easy death. No pain." Somehow, this information was coming through a stranger. In fact, even Lorraine had been caught off guard. She hadn't gone into trance as she was learning to do. Michael simply broke in and took over.

Now he was back, cutting in a second time: "Well, I got to be going," Michael said through Lorraine. "I got things to do." And he left.

This was Wally and Ardis's introduction to first-person paranormal. It was the first of several conversations they would have with Michael through Vic and Lorraine, and the beginning of an ongoing exploration into the invisible realms of spirit communication. It was January 1975.

Over the next few months, the couples got to know each other. When their teenage son Jerry moved out of their basement apartment, Wally and Ardis invited Vic and Lorraine, who had been living in their reflexology office, to make use of it on weekends. They would drive over from Rochester on Friday night and leave Monday morning, and as Wally puts it, "We'd have sessions. People would ask Vic and Lorraine to do things. And we'd be in on that."

Contacting dead relatives and friends, clearing entities from houses, leading guided tours through previous lives, and doing rescue missions (sending souls to the Light) were the kind of things people asked the Darrs to do. From the outset, Wally and Ardis were doing more than sitting in.

Wally's background in psychology and training as a therapist and counselor proved an easy adjunct to Lorraine's developing skills as a medium.

She'd been a third grade teacher. Vic had been a steel worker who got injured on the job and cured himself with reflexology in the hospital. He had fallen from a beam where he'd been pounding rivets and was told by physicians he would never walk again.

Vic refused the sentence. He had fallen before—from a tree as a child. He'd gone out of his body, after which he was suddenly able to render marvelous drawings—a miracle for which his teachers made him pay by accusing him of tracing.

So, this many years later, when doctors told him he would never walk again, Vic sat himself up in bed with a book on reflexology and worked on his feet until he walked out of there.

"Lorraine was just beginning to do automatic writing," Wally said, "and I think she was as surprised as we were when she came down the steps and Michael took over."

"Before that she had experienced many lower entities coming through and saying horrible things about her family, making threats, and so it frightened her to keep on doing automatic writing," Ardis said.

"She hadn't learned yet how to protect herself from negative spirit entities," said Wally.

"When they came down on weekends she would go into a trance and bring these like . . ."

"Xano."

"Xano in. And she would get up and assume this masculine position and her voice would go deep and it was interesting to watch her."

"You get used to it," said Wally, "knowing there's a different personality there. It's still Lorraine's body, but a different personality and maybe a different voice. Sometimes her voice was kind of a tinkly Chinese, very fragile, feminine. Sometimes it would be officious."

"She never knew who was coming through when she went into a trance."

"Sometimes she did."

"Sometimes she did."

"But, a lot of times people would just stumble onto the stage of her light, and be attracted to her light."

"They would stumble onto the stage of her light?" I asked.

He said yes. "Both she and Vic emanated a lot of light. Many times that's what attracts an earthbound spirit. That this station is like a beacon that pulls people in. Like Les K. the day he was killed."

Les K. was a colleague of Wally's who had driven through a railroad crossing guard on his way home from work. The train had hit his car at about one thirty in the afternoon. He died around four. By eight that evening, Les K. had stumbled, mumbling, into a session with Lorraine in trance.

As was standard, Wally had his tape recorder going. Lorraine was channeling the entity identified as Xano, whose words were coming through her in broken phrases divided by short pauses. Vic and Wally and Ardis found themselves leaning forward toward Lorraine for the duration of a very long pause. Finally, Lorraine's weight shifted in her body and her voice went up a notch, taking on the qualities of an anxious male.

LES K., SEPTEMBER 1, 1977
LORRAINE DARR IN TRANCE

Lorraine: *Wally, what happened? One moment I was working through a projected . . . theme . . . and then I was surrounded by many things . . . I remember no sounds.*

Wally: *What were you surrounded by?*

Lorraine: *Feelings of great love. Lights of varied colors, mostly white. Gentle strains of music . . . causing me to rest . . . causing this . . . quiet . . . state which I am . . . in.*

Wally: *Do you feel peaceful now? No pain?*

Lorraine: *One blinding instant of pain . . . and then it was released into this . . . feeling.*

Wally: *Is this Les? Are you Les?*

Lorraine: *Yes.*

Wally: *And you're wondering what happened.*

Les was a World War II vet who had been close to death several times. He and Wally had talked about life after death in the teachers' lounge.

Lorraine: *So strange. Yet I have all . . . faith . . . that I will understand.*

Wally: *Yes you will. We talked a few weeks ago about these sorts of things, if you recall.*

Lorraine: *This . . . came to me as I was resting.*

Wally: *Your memory of what we talked about came to you?*

Lorraine: *Pictures . . . flowed before me.*

Wally: *Uh huh?*

Lorraine: *Of things which had been said. I . . . don't remember being dead. Not . . . punishing. Not . . . bad. Not . . . painful. Just floating.*

Wally: *Just a very rapid transition.*

Lorraine: *As if . . . I slipped out. Popping like a watermelon seed.*

Wally: *And your awareness slipped out of your body, almost squirted out.*

Lorraine: *Yes.*

Wally: *And there was no pain?*

Lorraine: *No.*

Wally: *But lots of memories. And light. And peace and calm.*

Lorraine: *Many . . . people around me, some touching me.*

Wally: *People that you knew, Les? Before? People who had died previously?*

Lorraine: *I don't recognize . . . yet.*

Wally: *You don't see them clearly.*

Lorraine: *Very tired. They tell me I must rest.*

Wally: *Yes. Go ahead and rest and we hope to talk again.*

Lorraine: *Beautiful.*

Wally: *Do you have a message for Thelma?*

Lorraine: *Wherever I am . . . it is beautiful . . . lovely. I'm resting.*

Wally: *Would you like me to share that thought with Thelma?*

Lorraine: *She would understand.*

Wally: *All right. Go ahead and rest, Les. We'll be in touch.*

As it turned out, Thelma did *not* understand. She wanted nothing to do with Wally or this message from her husband on the so-called other side.

"Some people may have thought I'd gone off the deep end," Wally told me, and his eyes sparkled. Their work with Vic and Lorraine was beginning to get interesting.

The four of them were working as a unit. He and Ardis seemed to augment what Vic and Lorraine were doing. "I think I did verbally what they did mentally," Wally said. Vic was usually silent and seemed to be sending telepathic messages to entities while Wally talked out loud to them through Lorraine.

"At the time, Lorraine felt she had to be physically touching Vic or he had to be physically touching her, their feet, for the energy, for her to be able to maintain this space that she was in," Ardis said.

"Maintain the space?" I asked.

"To be in the psychic—the trance state. So she always had her foot up against Vic's foot."

"And she always had a gallon jug of water to drink from," Wally added. "For dehydration, which would leach out a lot of minerals if she didn't take supplements. It's hard work for a medium to turn over their body."

"And is that what she does? She turns over her body?"

"Lorraine steps back and the spirit takes over," he said.

"Her soul, her spirit, her—"

"Her etheric body. When she is in charge, her etheric body is congruent with her physical body. If she pulls her etheric body back and he moves his etheric body in, then the spirit can use her vocal chords to speak through."

Lorraine refers to this period of her life as "the time of my allowing."

"It was Vic, of course, who could see the entities in the room," Ardis said. "He'd see shapes and have the knowledge of who was there."

It was Vic who had seen Michael that first day. "There's been a young one standing right beside Ardis ever since I started," Vic had said.

2

Michael Knew He Was Dead

MICHAEL KNEW HE WAS DEAD. In fact, Michael's first words out of Lorraine Darr's mouth were words of reassurance to his parents that he was still around and that his death had been an easy one. In subsequent visits, Michael talked about the work he was doing. He was greeting new arrivals, particularly children, and orienting them to their new surroundings, showing them around. He had made a smooth transition into the afterlife and was busy learning things.

The second time Michael spoke through Lorraine, Wally got him on tape.

MICHAEL JOHNSTON, JANUARY 29, 1976
LORRAINE DARR IN TRANCE

Lorraine: *We have a lot of fun and I know a lot of people. A lot of kids. They sure need a lot of attention sometimes.*

It's different over here now, that's the funny part. You don't learn by doing things. You learn by seeing. It's different.

We have classes. These teachers are real nice. You have to learn to operate a little differently here. But, once you get the hang of it, it's pretty good.

■   ■   ■

Much of Wally's work in the Counseling/Education Department at Winona State was designing courses that kept up with his developing interests in death and dying, life after death, and psychic phenomena. With materials developed for his course called Living with Dying, Wally went to the High Rise Senior Center to begin a group. The one person who came every week to that group was a woman named Marion Ayers. Months after the group broke up, in June of the same year Wally met Vic and Lorraine, Marion Ayers died.

"Vic and Lorraine were there. It was probably Thursday night, and I had just come by the Fawcett Funeral Home and there was a visitation and a lot of cars," Wally told me. "I came home and read the paper and here's her death."

Wally handed me a copy of an obituary notice from the *Winona Daily News*:

> June 11, 1975, Mrs. Marion Ayers, age 79, died at 5:20 Tuesday at Community Memorial Hospital, after a month of illness. She was born in England, 1896, lived in Winona most of her life. Married Lee Ayers in 1917 in Chicago, who died in 1968. She was a member of First Church of Christ Science, and a past First Reader of the Church and a member of the . . .

"I turned to Vic and said, 'hey, Vic, can you send some energy to her?'"

Vic did.

Six days later, Marion Ayers started coming to Lorraine

through automatic writing. Wally handed me a folder of type-written pages and I began to read out loud:

> **Marion Ayers:** *I'm so grateful to have received thought healing from your friend. It enabled me to rest more fully since I spoke to you and came before you all. That was so peculiar a feeling for me to stand before Wally and he did not see me. That brought me the realization I really have a body no longer, as it is unnecessary, and the freedom this brings one's soul is just great. There are many good souls here with the new arrivals, helping with love to make the waking a pleasant thing. Also to help those who do not believe they are here as spirits but think they are dreaming. Much more should be known concerning death, as we discussed.*

"We talked about this at the retirement center," Wally said. "How to let people know what's going to happen when they die."

I went on.

> **Marion Ayers:** *I simply went to sleep. In pain, true, but just closed my eyes with the thought, 'I am going to God.' And there was a doorway a short way away, which I walked over to and opened.*

"This is that boundary line that we always talk about in the near death experience," Wally said. "This really confirms that the near death is an actual prelude. It's real."

I kept reading.

> **Marion Ayers:** *I'm considering, Wally, whether the single biggest factor to know before death may be the fact that*

one goes in love, gently held in the loving arms of God, knowing that there is no fear. Probably the greatest shock is knowing you all cannot see us anymore with your earth eyes. This seems to give some the feeling of being lost. It is taken care of as we learn to know ourselves with no earthly body for covering.

Many people, knowing so little or nothing of the life after death, have the mistaken notion that there is nothing. So, therefore, they prepare nothing in advance. The best way to be ready for the transformation to spirit is accepting that there is an afterlife, learning about it, discussing it with friends.

When the spirit body arrives after the separation from the physical, the cord, which formerly had held the spirit body near the physical body is automatically severed by the knowing thought of death. The cord is a tangible thing of infinite strength. It is seldom seen or felt but serves its purpose.

"The knowing thought of death?" I asked Wally.

"The knowing thought, apparently, severs the cord," he said.

"Her thought? Death's thought?"

"Your own thought of death, that knowing that you've crossed the ditch, the bridge, the doorway, river, chasm. Once you have that knowing, once you know," Wally said, "that's it."

Marion Ayers: *Although one wakes and notices what takes place around him, he is not really active for a time. The major difference is that one needs to learn that there is no Earth Time. You have all eternity, and knowing this brings such a feeling of peace to one's soul. One learns to walk all over again. It is simply a matter of using the* *mind and one's body of the now state. To not have muscles for movement seems not to matter. The movement is as a floating sensation in slow motion. A grand feeling and really fun learning.*

"She likes this floating around," Wally grinned.

Marion Ayers: *The only hell there is exists in the mind of the person. If one believes they will go to the region they call hell, he will go there. And stay there. Only then will he be able-with help-to proceed on.*

"'As a man thinketh, so he is,'" Wally quoted.

Marion Ayers: *Wally, you are so right concerning the need to know what our mind can do and is equipped to do from birth, and we do not recognize it.*

We are now learning to be aware that the new state is of the spirit. We are learning to move and to think and to be without the help of a physical body. A group of souls meets under a tree and enjoys nature while learning about one's true self, the spirit. The spirit enables us to exist here. The physical body is not a part of us any longer. So, the spirit and ego must complete their learning.

This knowing oneself within can be done on earth easier than here. People must know this and help prepare for the transformation of one's soul. This is the reason I feel the need to say these things and for them to be used as teaching by not only you, Wally, but many people. We make a good team. You there and myself and others here.

Over forty-four days Marion Ayers delivered fourteen messages. She ended her last one with this:

> **Marion Ayers**: *One is totally in God here and it is a freer life.*
> *One to look forward to and not dread. It is a joy to work*
> *and learn when love is allowed to carry one every*
> *moment, to be useful to earth souls and friends here until*
> *such time as the soul is ready to leave here for further*
> *learning. Joy to the world, one and all. Marion Ayers.*

■   ■   ■

Ten months later, the man who had brought Wally and Ardis
and Vic and Lorraine together, Brother Joel Nelson, went into
the hospital. Since they met, Wally had gotten to know Brother
Joel, had taken his mind control class at St. Mary's, and
"Brother Joel would feed me materials and books much the
way I feed materials to people now."

Wally went to see him at the hospital. "I was alone there with
him, and he said, 'Wally, will you help me take out my teeth?' So,
I helped him get his dentures out. Rinsed them, scrubbed them
off, and put them in a drawer." Brother Joel knew he was dying.
He was ready to go. He decided to stop eating. He wouldn't need
his teeth. Three days later, Brother Joel passed on, crossed over,
checked out, transitioned, met his maker, graduated, kicked the
bucket, bit the dust, and bought the farm.

Six days after that, on May 1, 1976, Brother Joel came
through Lorraine in trance.

"There is a freedom felt," he said through Lorraine. "A joy
in the very impulses around us."

He had enjoyed the various gatherings of friends after his
passing, he said, but "the many expressions of my worth I don't
feel justified in claiming." He went on:

Lorraine: *There is a different relationship, which I must master yet, to enable my being to get about easier. I feel that I have done it before, and in that feeling I place the image and will learn this way.*

This area we are a part of now is very beautiful. A delicate blue with golden light which seems to come from everywhere. There are many wise, understanding souls here who have welcomed me with their touch. I feel very excited over the coming days. There, I used a term from habit, as I know there are no "days" here—only eternal forever.

In the adjustment we are going through, the other souls and myself will leave many things behind. The appearance of our bodies is startling. I just had pictured within me how I thought I would look. As yet I appear just as I was. Maybe this is necessary for a time.

We rest often, listen to music, soft strains of music unlike any that I have heard. The music itself seems to enable the soul to adjust and really see well. The various tones affect parts of me. It is all very comfortable.

Then, "Peace, my beloved friends. I love you. I must go."

Brother Joel not only knew he was dead, he had known he was dying. He had prepared for death. And, as with Michael Johnston and Marion Ayers, he had made a smooth transition and was learning and growing and mastering the methods of life on the other side.

But many who die do not know they are dead.

3

Ghost Counseling

MARK GRECO NEVER KNEW WHAT HIT HIM. He had stopped to help somebody whose car had broken down on the side of the road. When he got out of his car, he apparently stood in front of his own taillights and was hit and killed and for two earth years had been stuck in a dreamscape generated by his own confusion. His physical body had been carried away. His car was towed. His death was mourned. But Mark's spirit body had frozen in his final glimpse of physical reality, is how Wally describes it. Until a friend, Tony, asked Vic and Lorraine to try to contact him.

SEPTEMBER 30, 1977, AT A FARM HOME NEAR WESTBY, WISCONSIN LORRAINE DARR IN TRANCE

Lorraine: *Feels good, I'm here, I'm here, hey, I'm here. God, do I hurt. Yes. Why did I get out of the car? Someone needed help. Help. Help. Strange place. Nobody talks to you. They just look at you and smile. They don't know how I'm feeling.*

Wally: *How do you feel?*

Lorraine: *I guess I'm angry more than I hurt. For some reason, the hurt isn't there. It's like being popped right out of a grape skin. One minute one place, and the next minute, whole different thing.*

Wally: *You're angry about where you are, Mark?*

Lorraine: *I feel like I ought to know why I came, but I just can't get a hold of it. I just can't see.*

Wally: *It's very confusing to you. Is it that you can't see why you popped out? Or you can't see why you're here now?*

Lorraine: *I've been just walking around, watching and listening, and somebody's been beside me. I know somebody's been beside me but I can't talk to them. They've just been beside me.*

Wally: *You can't make them understand.*

Lorraine: *It's not that I wanted to stay. It's just, it was so fast.*

Wally: *You're angry about how fast it was and how confusing it is?*

Lorraine: *I seem to have been many places. One place, there was just music. Wasn't really what I liked. But it just was there. And it was all right. And then there was another place, different, real different. I guess it's because when I reach out to touch people, they aren't there. That's it. They aren't there. But they are.*

Wally: *You try to make contact, but you can't.*

Lorraine: *I can see them, but when I reach out, I don't touch anything.*

"Here's a very typical hand going through the body," Wally pipes in as the tape plays.

Lorraine: *How come they don't know I'm here? Maybe that's why nobody paid any attention. Except the one beside me.*

Wally stops the tape. "Here's this guide coming along beside him trying to get his attention and he's still focusing on the physical reality. If he'd just shift and look out *through* the window—"

"Instead of looking at the spot *on* the window," I finish his thought. It's a good metaphor. One he's used before. Wally nods and turns the tape recorder back on.

Wally: *Maybe they can't see you, Mark.*
Lorraine: *Well.*
Wally: *Are you aware that you no longer have your physical body?*
Lorraine: *I just thought I did.*
Wally: *You can see it but no one else can see it. Is that right?*
Lorraine: *Well, I have it, I just thought everybody saw it.*
Wally: *You feel like you have a body and to you, you look like you have a body, but nobody can see your body. That's why everybody just walks by and just ignores you. God, that makes you angry, too.*
Lorraine: *Well, man, I always wondered what was going on.*
Wally: *They look where you are and they can't see you.*
Vic: *Mark, were you not aware that you were dead?*
Lorraine: *I didn't know what happened because I can see where I was and I can see people, and yet they didn't hear me, either. And then I just sort of went to sleep. Haven't tried to do much of anything.*

Wally: *Feeling a little more relaxed now?*

Lorraine: *I see somebody right over there and they're look-ing right at me and smiling. I wonder. I'm going to walk over. He's bowing. I look like she does. Oh, yeah, that's what it said in the music.*

Wally: *What did it say in the music, Mark?*

Lorraine: *You'll feel and see differently. I really don't have it any more. Just like it said in the music, they seem to get along just fine. So, I guess I can. Hm. These people, they look just like me.*

Wally: *So you're not alone anymore.*

Lorraine: *Uh huh.*

"Now he's tuning into *that* reality," Wally said.

Wally: *There are others like you around. They can see you. That feels good. They notice you.*

Lorraine: *One of them is saying come with me, come with me. We must go and learn.*

Wally: *Mark, is there someone you love very much who has died? Can you think of anyone?*

Lorraine: *I love my family.*

Wally: *Some of your family, have they died?*

Lorraine: *Haven't seen them.*

Wally: *Can you call to them?*

Lorraine: *People all over here now.*

Wally: *Uh huh. Is there something you would like for me to do for you here?*

Lorraine: *Just think about me. I just seem like to be in kind of a mist. Oh, I remember what happened. And yet I don't feel like I did when I first came back here and started talking to you. But it's just sort of misty. They* keep saying, *"You will know, you'll know, you'll under-stand, don't feel bad, don't feel bad." I'm comfortable. It's like I'm me but I'm not me and it's kind of strange. I have to go. Something is just compelling me to go. "Never grieve for those who are lost." This one beside me just told me this. I'm going to look around and see what I can see. It's going to be all right. It's going to be all right.*

Wally: *Sounds interesting. Maybe when you get acquainted around, you can come back and share with us.*

Lorraine: *The car just faded away.*

Wally: *The car?*

Lorraine: *It's gone now. It's been by me. It's gone now. Well, strange place. We're going. I just realized, I'm not walking. We're all sort of floating along.*

Wally: *That sounds exciting.*

Lorraine: *Good. The one beside me just said this is the usual manner of movement, which we will help you learn better. I guess I have a lot to do. Thank you. Thank you for bringing me. I don't know how you did it, but it was just like I was drawn, like a piece of string. I'm glad.*

Wally: *I'm glad, too, that you're comfortable now.*

Lorraine: *So long. Strange, but it's been very nice. I really feel good. So long.*

Wally: *Good night.*

Lorraine: *So long.*

Whatever he may or may not have believed would happen at the moment of death, Mark Greco's death had blindsided him. Like being popped out of a grape skin into a strange place where nobody talks to you. He hears music, doesn't like it, reaches out to people "and they aren't there." He senses someone is beside him—Wally thinks this is a guide—but Mark's attention is focused on the physical world.

Wally gets Mark to realize that he is dead. That his physical body is gone. Mark is alive within his spirit body now and there is someone beside him who is ready to help.

"Oh, yeah, that's what it said in the music."

Mark relaxes enough to look around and gradually tune in to the reality of the spirit world, where those around him have no physical bodies either and yet "seem to get along just fine." One says, "Come with me, we must go and learn."

The mist lifts. The dreamscape he's been trapped in—by the roadside, by the car—fades away. Mark moves on.

■   ■   ■

"You are a ghost counselor," I tell Wally.

Wally brightens. "I'm counseling, yes, this is the way I see it. I'm the counselor, and I can't see them, but they can respond to me through Lorraine and I can talk to them, and so this is a counseling session and the earthbound spirit is my client, that I'm working for, to help them understand where they are and what is happening."

Colleagues

WE SIT IN WALLY'S OFFICE STACKED HIGH WITH BOOKS and videos. A file cabinet stands crammed with folders going back into the sixties. We've been reading transcripts and listening to tapes. Cassette recordings of their work with Vic and Lorraine from 1975 to 1981 still live unceremoniously in two shoeboxes in the closet. Wally puts Mark Greco's tape back into one of these and sits, drifting, thinking. He separates himself from me. I look out the window.

In the backyard, twenty feet from the house, stands a 106-foot Sequoia Redwood tree. Its circumference at shoulder height is eighteen feet. The shadow of its shape—a perfect inverted cone—daily crosses the lawns and houses of the neighborhood like the shadow of the blade of a sundial.

"I am trying to remember what I knew about life after death."

I turn. "At the time, you mean."

"At the time, yes," he says. "I know I had Helen Wambach's book."

Helen Wambach was a psychologist and teacher who used time regression hypnosis with large groups of people. Her research revealed large-scale memory of past lives among her subjects. *Reliving Past Lives* explores the notion that consciousness exists outside the body before the body is formed, that we keep coming back, and that we may even choose our parents. The Bantam mass market edition (published in 1978) sits beside her second book, *Life Before Life* (1979), in a section of books about reincarnation on Wally's shelves.

But before Helen Wambach there was Elisabeth Kubler-Ross, who became famous for her study of the psychology of death when *Life* magazine featured her in 1969. "Johnny Cash was on the cover of that issue," Wally tells me. "I still have it around here somewhere."

Swiss-born, one of triplets, Kubler-Ross addressed the taboo of death head-on in her book *On Death and Dying* by interviewing hundreds of terminally ill patients on the topic of being terminally ill. She found this direct approach almost completely lacking in Western medicine and medical training. At a time when the truth of patient diagnoses was often routinely being kept from both patients and family, she asked why. Was it for the mental well-being of the patient? Of the family? Or because some physicians had problems of their own in dealing with the realities of death? This is the book in which she identified the now famous five stages of death—denial and isolation, anger, bargaining, depression, and acceptance.

Wally invited Kubler-Ross to Winona for a five-day seminar. Her work held special interest for him. His course in Living with Dying featured her book, which had inspired his pamphlet, "End of Life Planning—Things to Have Ready at Death." Your will, donor information, information for the obit, bank account, life insurance. Do you want cremation or a burial? Open casket? Closed casket? Do you want to be buried with your jewelry? Do you want to wear your glasses?

Where do you want to die? Who do you want to have with you when you die?

"And who do you want to have meet you on the other side?" Wally asks. "Or, would you like to find somebody to teach you to go out of your body? Have a field trip to see what it's like over there? Maybe you'd like to think about what you would like to do when you get there. Have a tour. Because all these things are available."

Sometimes if his Living with Dying group was "small enough and pretty advanced," he would ask his students if they'd like to try to contact a relative that they might have unfinished business with. "What do you wish you'd said to them before they died?" he would ask. And Vic and Lorraine would come in. Sometimes the overheads would flicker. Often contact was made.

"But back in '74," I ask him, "before you met Vic and Lorraine, what did you know?"

"I knew Elmer Green's work in biofeedback," he answers.

Wally had gone to Vermillion, South Dakota, on a National Defense Education Act fellowship in 1964. Three years later, he had his Masters and a Doctorate in Educational Psychology and Guidance. The idea of the NDEA was to guide bright students into science and math and foreign languages so that the U. S. could catch up with the Russians who were first to put an orbiting satellite into space—*Sputnik*, in October of 1957.

"Because the Russians were bent on global domination, as I understand it," I say.

"Yeah, they taught us how," he answers. "Choose your enemy carefully because you're bound to emulate them."

Wally's job was teaching counseling theories, so he had to keep up on all the new therapies. In the late sixties and early seventies, there was an explosion of different ways of working with people. Past Life Therapy, Cognitive Therapy, Rational Emotive Therapy, Irrational Belief Therapy. He had a book around there somewhere that had forty different therapies listed and described. Frank Farrelly, for instance, from Wisconsin, stumbled into Provocative Therapy and one day simply began insulting his clients. With great results.

Wally had entered the field as the Behaviorism of John B. Watson and B. F. Skinner was giving way to the client-centered therapies of Carl Rogers and Abraham Maslow. Actually, he told me there were three major psychologies. Freudian, "where the id runs the show and the ego tries to control it and the superego makes you feel guilty if it doesn't." Behaviorism, which concerned itself with how to control the behavior of others through conditioning, punishment, and rewards. "But who gets to decide whose behavior is controlled and punished and rewarded?" Wally asked.

Then humanism, or Third Force Psychology, "where you've got people with choices, instead of being controlled from the inside by the id or from the outside by the manipulator. You may even have a spark of the divine."

Abraham Maslow was the first to study healthy human beings instead of "going through all of the sicknesses. Maslow wrote about self-actualized people. And he found there is goodness in the id. Whoever heard of such a thing? See, this was totally un-Freudian."

Humanism led to Transpersonal Psychology, "which is the full-fledged admission of spirituality being part of it" and where self-concept and self-esteem became an object of study. "Self-concept is what you believe about yourself, and your self-esteem is the feeling that that belief creates."

This dove-tailed into the work of Prescott Lecky, whose thesis was that what you believe about yourself—whether true or false—becomes the boundaries within which you live your life. To live inconsistently with these beliefs about yourself will cause discomfort.

Wally looked at everything—"Whatever works."—and even though he'd been hired at Winona State, which was a Humanist school, he used a relaxation tape developed by a South African behaviorist to work with clients who were phobic about spiders, frogs, and snakes.

The tape employed a series of positive statements similar to the Autogenic Training statements originated by German cardiologist Johannes Shultz as a visualization aid to lessen the risk of heart attacks among his clients. "I feel quite quiet. I am beginning to feel quite relaxed." Wally discovered the work of Shultz through Elmer Green.

The genius of Elmer Green is that he combined Shultz's self-induced training statements with his own work in biofeedback.

> Biofeedback is the feedback of biological information to a person. It is the continuous monitoring, amplifying, and displaying to a person (usually by a needle on a meter, or by a light or a tone) of an ongoing internal physiological process, such as muscle tension, temperature, heart behavior, or brain rhythm. (Green, *The Ozawkie Book of the Dead*)

Muscle tension, body temperature, heart behavior, and brain rhythm are all physiological processes governed by the autonomic nervous system. Medical textbooks at the time said that voluntary control of the autonomic nervous system was impossible.

But Elmer Green knew enough about Eastern yogic traditions to know that the difference between voluntary and involuntary was a matter of degree.

By monitoring their biological feedback through electromyogram (EMG) and electroencephalogram (EEG) and temperature training machines while in a relaxed state and visualizing the desired result, his subjects learned to lower their heart rate, alter their brain waves, and change their flow of blood.

"Elmer Green found out that when you say 'My hands are warm,' your hands get warm," Wally told me. "Your body responds to what you hold in your mind."

When you give someone a sugar pill to kill pain, and the person who takes it believes the pill will kill the pain, and the pain goes away, this is known as the placebo effect. "It generates endorphins," Wally said. "You've got an expectation creating a physiological effect. The belief, the expectation, releases the endorphins and the pain goes away."

Wally had known about the placebo effect for many years, but no one knew about endorphins until when?

"Late seventies, early eighties maybe. It was a shock to the medical community when they found out that this wasn't just the patient trying to please the examiner. That's what placebo means. The desire to please. No. A placebo kills the pain because it generates endorphins. *This is an actual physical substance that's created by a mental expectation*," Wally said.

This is mind over matter. This is the power of belief. This is what Elmer Green proved when he demonstrated that our minds penetrate every cell in our body and what Cleve Backster means when he says that our cells "talk" to each other and that the cells of one species even talk to the cells of other species.

All this intrigued the hell out of Wally. He dove into biofeedback in March of '74, took his training in Topeka with Elmer and Alyce Green, qualified himself to teach it, and returned to Minnesota, where he ordered three temperature trainers, two

EMGs, and an EEG through the college. By summer, he had his own equipment. By fall, he was teaching a course on biofeedback and relaxation and was using biofeedback as he counseled half-time at the university counseling center.

■   ■   ■

"You want this tight enough so that it doesn't get away from you," he tells me. "You're at 81, 82 point one, two, 82 point three, four . . . . see this little light here moving?"

The temperature trainer is a small blue box. Wally fit the contact to my fingertip with a fuzzy cutoff glove. The idea is to relax enough to keep the light moving to the right.

I'm in Wally's office—November, 2002. But I have done this in the dim past. I don't remember when.

"Sit up straight with your feet flat on the floor," he tells me. "Balance your head on your spine so that you're neither falling forward nor backward. Allow your hands to rest in your lap, palms up, fingers curled naturally. You're at 86 point seven. As I read these phrases, take time to imagine and feel the relaxation of each part of the body as you silently repeat these phrases to yourself. First we'll be quieting the body."

I repeat after him:

I am beginning to feel quite relaxed.

My feet feel heavy and relaxed.

My ankles, my knees, and my hips feel heavy and relaxed and comfortable.

The whole central part of my body feels relaxed and quiet.

My hands and arms feel heavy, relaxed, and comfortable.

I lower my shoulders slightly and feel them relax.

I roll my head gently and relax the tight spots in my neck.

I allow my jaw to go limp and feel it sag slightly.

My forehead feels smooth, cool, and relaxed.

My whole body feels quiet and comfortable and relaxed.

And now we'll be quieting the emotions. I am quiet and relaxed.

Wally goes on with statements to quiet my emotions. He then continues with statements to quiet my mind.

"You're at 91 point one, point two, three. Let your jaw sag, let your shoulders go down, visualize blood flowing to your hands, 91 point five. Focus on the light, move the light to the right."

Moments pass.

"Just continue to move the red light to the right."

More moments pass.

I am no longer in Portland, Oregon.

Wally's office dissolves into a motel room in Omaha, summer 1974.

The drapes are drawn and the room is full of soft blue light. Wally brought his temperature trainer to the Johnston family reunion, and his youngest child, Julie, maybe six years old, is giggling with her fingers cuffed in the fuzzy cutoff glove. Her eyes sparkle as she effortlessly makes the red light jumpfrog to the right. Her numbers shoot up into the very high 90s.

"How do you do that?" I ask her, amazed.

"It's easy. I just see myself flying into the sun and the closer I get, the warmer my hands get."

Imaging is easy for Julie. She hasn't been on the planet long and her parents have refrained from telling her what is and isn't true, what is and isn't possible. Her parents are in the process of finding that out for themselves, so it's been natural to include her in their sessions with Vic and Lorraine.

One day, she'll jump up on stage with Israeli psychic Uri Geller. She'll hold a spoon he bends with the power of his mind and be witness to a pile of broken watches chirping back to life.

"Keys were bending in people's pockets," Wally told me. "Geller had twelve hundred people chanting: 'work, work, work, work.' These are *words*—that change reality."

Julie held a big, old, Roman-numeral, thick-lens gold watch. "I think it had an elk engraved on the back like my dad's did, only his was silver. And the darned thing started working. About eighty percent of the watches there started working. Some of them, they said, had parts missing."

A migraine wedge of noonday sun cuts into the Omaha motel room. Ruth enters wearing flip-flops, a swimsuit, and a towel. Julie shoots out past her and the door falls shut. Again, hushed blue light as angles soften. Again, a quiet vibration of love.

Ruth is Wally's youngest sister, my aunt. Square shoulders, late forties, she is a psychiatric nurse and director of psychiatric nursing at Wayne State in Detroit. Wally wires her up to the temperature trainer and she begins to tune into the back and forth of her thoughts and feelings as they affect the movement of the small red light.

Ruth's professional background is both medical and academic. Like her older brother she holds advanced degrees, but is less inclined than Wally is to believe in the far-out, "the woo-woo stuff," he calls it. Yet she has seen enough of doctors and Western medicine to know there is a gap between how science describes things and how things may be. Right now she's finding out that the machine she is on is proof of the lie she was taught in nurse's training. The body's autonomic processes *can* be influenced by conscious intervention.

As she "plays with it," some of the images and feelings Ruth thought would bring fear, hence constrict blood flow and cause her hands to cool, aren't having that effect. A couple times, thoughts she doesn't expect to trigger fear, do just that.

Ruth is growing more curious about "this mind/body bit," as she calls it, not just because of Wally, but also since the phantom pregnancy at work.

A psychiatric patient on the ward began behaving as if she were pregnant. The young woman manifested physical symptoms including interrupted menses, distension of the belly, even morning sickness. She, herself, was convinced that she was pregnant. She wasn't. It was psychogenic—"originating within the mind, of psychological rather than physical origin."

"Ruth always was suspicious that the mind had a lot to do with the body," Wally told me, "and when she ran into biofeedback in '74, it gave her documentation of the effects of it. So, that was part of her opening. And that's what she appreciates about biofeedback—it was a bridge between our fetish, almost, with science and the measurable, and the *un*measurable."

The major influence on Ruth's underlying beliefs at the time was her friend and mentor, nursing theorist Dr. Martha Rogers, whose book, *An Introduction to the Theoretical Basis of Nursing* (1970), helped revolutionize the field of nursing and usher in what has since become known as the Holistic Nursing Movement.

It was under Rogers, longtime director of graduate nursing at NYU, that Dolores Kreiger developed the energetic healing modality known as Therapeutic Touch. TT is based, in part, on the system of beliefs advanced by Rogers.

Among Martha Rogers's beliefs are:

- Man is an energy field, an open system, coextensive with the universe.
- Man and the environment are continuously exchanging matter and energy.
- The life process evolves irreversibly and unidirectionally along the time-space continuum.
- There is no regression; there is only progress.

"Meaning what?" I asked Ruth close to thirty years later.

"That we don't wind down. We get better, continuously moving and changing and growing and healing. This is the opposite of entropy. Negentropy, she called it. With entropy, aging was inevitable deterioration, dementia, and so forth. Negentropy was a whole different organization of ideas. You begin to see that aging is a developmental process, not an illness. It becomes easier to see more positive things happening. And an awful lot of people who would have gone down the tubes along with the expectation that that's what you're supposed to do began to expect something else—to live longer, move around. The whole notion of aging has undergone a tremendous change.

"But when Rogers published her book in 1970, most of nursing was thinking, 'This woman's on the sauce; she's out of it.' I read the thing and thought, 'Thank God here's somebody who's thinking beyond where we're stuck.' It was so refreshing to me. But I didn't understand enough of the physics to understand it all. It just resonated and I knew it was right, but I didn't have the background and I didn't have the time to explore it."

Ruth wouldn't find time to explore it for many years. But this moment in August of 1974 remains outside time.

The three of us sit in a motel room in Omaha.

Ruth's face is calm, without a ripple, eyes closed, jaw slack.

Wally watches her.

I watch them both.

A delicate blue with golden light seems to come from everywhere.

Years later, Wally would tell me with pride that this was the moment he and Ruth "became colleagues."

5

How Many Are There?

APRIL 26, 1980, SEXTONVILLE, WISCONSIN
LORRAINE DARR IN TRANCE

Wally: *Why do you remain?*

Lorraine: *This is my home. Where else should I go? I like this place . . . Good place. Good place.*

Wally: *You built this yourself, Ezra?*

Lorraine: *Stone by stone.*

Wally: *Put a lot of effort into it.*

Lorraine: *Two rooms. Fireplace. It's been good.*

Wally: *You've liked it. Do you ever get lonely here?*

Lorraine: *Never. There's always things to do.*

Wally: *What sorts of things, Ezra?*

Lorraine: *I take long walks . . . I work the field . . . I bake bread. . . . But these sounds. I don't understand what's happening . . . of late . . . I seem to hear . . . sounds. . . .*

Wally: *It's confusing, I guess.*

Lorraine: *Sometimes my home doesn't look like my home. And I'm in a different place.*

Wally: *You mean like a wood house instead of a stone house?*

Lorraine: *Well . . . a house of logs . . . fixed . . . every wall. Even whitewashed inside. It seems as if I go back and forth. Someone tries to talk to me. And . . . I don't see anybody.*

Wally: *But you feel somebody is around.*

Lorraine: *Somebody is saying, "It's time to go, it's time to go."*

Wally: *You're wondering where to go?*

Lorraine: *No, why I should go. . . . (Sigh) Now there are more. More and more . . . people . . . coming into my little home saying it's time to go.*

Wally: *Are you aware that you are dead, Ezra? You are on the other side. But living in two different houses that were once here.*

Lorraine: *That may be the answer.*

Wally: *That's why you were confused?*

Lorraine: *Why . . . I could never . . . get people to listen.*

Wally: *They couldn't see you, Ezra. But you could see them.*

Lorraine: *I'm real!*

Wally: *You're dead but you're still real, Ezra.*

Lorraine: *I tried to eat . . . and my hand . . . went through the food. Didn't understand.*

Wally: *You don't need food now, Ezra. You don't have a body to feed. You look down and it looks like you have a body, but you don't have to feed that body. I'll bet you don't get hot or cold anymore, either, do you?*

Lorraine: *No. Haven't made the fire for a long time.*

Wally: *No, you can walk out in the snow barefoot. That's a different body you're in now, Ezra. You've left your old physical body. And it's kind of confusing.*

Lorraine: *Well . . . praise me . . . my . . . all right, it's time to go.*

Wally: *Do you want to call to somebody that you know and love? A mother? A father? Grandparent?*

Lorraine: *No, these are my friends.*

Wally: *You already see them, huh?*

Lorraine: *Yes.*

Wally: *They've come for you. Okay, why don't you go with them toward the Light. And you can be released from the stone house or the log house or wherever you've been trapped all this time.*

Lorraine: *(Sigh) . . . I don't hurt anymore.*

Wally: *Your shoulder's better.*

Lorraine: *It doesn't hurt.*

Wally: *What a relief.*

Lorraine: *It's still there. But it doesn't hurt.*

Wally: *It's a different kind of body that doesn't hurt. When you let go of it.*

Lorraine: *Hmm.*

Wally: *Sounds like an improvement to you, doesn't it?*

Lorraine: *I don't know.*

Wally: *(Laughs) Still strange.*

Lorraine: *Well, I have to go.*

Wally: *Before you go, will you tell us your last name, Ezra? And maybe what year it is?*

Lorraine: *Ezra Barrens . . . 1782.*

Wally: *Ezra Barrens, 1782. Good to know you. Go in peace.*

According to Wally, Ezra Barrens had been stuck in a thought form reality for two hundred years. He'd been hovering in the dreamscape of a house he had built with his own hands and knew every inch of, a house with which he was completely identified. But the house no longer stood.

"This is what Vic runs into," said Wally. "He may have three different houses in one place and different people moving in and out in their own reality and not knowing that there's another house that was there before then and another house after that."

Ezra Barrens was dead and did not know it.

He'd been drawn to the light of Vic and Lorraine, and Wally was able to persuade him to turn away from the physical world, to join friends who gathered on the other side, and to move off into the spirit world toward the Light of whatever came next.

"How many are there like Ezra Barrens?" I ask Wally. "Like Mark Greco? Like Les K.? How many people die and do not know they are dead?"

Wally gives me his back, doesn't answer, leaves the room. He's gone looking for a book. I turn the tape recorder on.

On that same day in 1980 when Wally counseled Ezra Barrens in Wisconsin, four other entities also came through Lorraine. One was a woman named Hannah they found sweeping with a broom. As I listen, Lorraine's voice slides into a higher register, assuming an accent I can't quite place:

Lorraine: *Go on with ye now; can't you see I'm busy? You're in my way, get out of my way! I have to clean this place!*

Wally: *You sound like a hard worker, Hannah.*

Lorraine: *What else is there?*

Wally: *Just work work work?*

Loraine: *That's all I know.*

Wally: *Who do you work for, Hannah?*

Lorraine: *Don't ask. I work for evil people. I have to work. I work fast and I do not look over my shoulder.*

Wally: *You mind your own business, hm?*

Lorraine: *I hear nothing. And I see nothing. And my work is good.*

Wally: *And as long as you work hard and mind your own business, then you feel safe? Even though you work for evil people?*

Lorraine: *God . . . will . . . take care of them.*

Wally: *Who is them?*

Lorraine: *I know nothing.*

Wally: *Would you like to move from this place, Hannah? Would you like to put your broom down? I bet you feel like you've been sweeping forever.*

Lorraine: *What else shall I do?*

Wally: *Would you like to get reunited with your family? Did you know your mother? Your father?*

Lorraine: *(Sigh) They gave me to work.*

Wally: *They gave you away? Was there anyone you loved?*

Lorraine: *My brother.*

Wally: *Your brother. What was his name, Hannah?*

Lorraine: *Ethan.*

Wally: *Ethan. Would you turn away from us and turn away from your broom, picture Ethan's face in your mind, and then call to Ethan. Call "Ethan" and wait for him.*

Lorraine: *(Long pause) . . . Hm . . . it's been so long since I went away from you. . . . Oh . . . you are . . . handsome. Is it really you, Ethan? . . . Oh. . . . Yes . . . I'll come. . . . Glad to leave. Oh, so glad to leave.*

Wally: *Feels good to stop sweeping, doesn't it, Hannah? Such a relief.*

Lorraine: *And I don't have to open the door . . . for those filthy men.*

On that same tape, in addition to Hannah, there is a man named Carl whose entire family perished from fever in three days. Carl is looking for Anna, his wife. There is also a farmer named Ora who keeps waiting for a woman named Teresa to return from a building that never stops burning. And there is Lonzo, a sailor stuck looking for his trunk.

> **Lorraine:** *The trunk I had on two voyages . . . Sailing the South Seas. Oh, what a beautiful . . . horrible place . . . You work yourself to death and you drop in a heap to sleep. And you work yourself to death the next day. Oh, but the ports are fun (Laughs) . . . if you don't get caught.*
>
> **Wally:** *When was this you did this, Lonzo?*
>
> **Lorraine:** *1632. . . . Oh, the vessels were beautiful. And the wind so free. And the water talks to you . . . and sometimes it takes you. Just miss your step . . . and it takes you. And you play the game. You'll not get me today. And you watch your step.*
>
> **Wally:** *You outsmart the ocean one day at a time, hm?*
>
> **Lorraine:** *This way I lived for several voyages.*
>
> **Wally:** *Uh huh. How do you happen to be here?*
>
> **Lorraine:** *I decided . . . to find me trunk. It had a shirt I wanted to feel. It had a book with beautiful pictures . . . of me home . . . It had a necklace of me mother's . . . and I loved it. Granny gave it to me . . . And the men they laughed. Hah! Look at that! Look at him! Keepin' his mother's necklace! Crazy! But I wasn't crazy. She talked to me from the necklace. She helped . . . when there was no food and when the ship was becalmed and people*

*died like flies . . . and I said I will not die. I will get back
to port. I will not die here in this . . . hot muck! And I
didn't!*

Wally reenters the office with the book he's been looking for
and starts to read out loud:

> For one who was sure that death was the end of all exis-
> tence, it is an even greater surprise to find himself still
> living while at the same time he can see his own body
> on the bed beside him. (Smith, *The Book of James*)

Wally interrupts himself. "Somewhere in here he describes a
dark gray cloud around the planet earth that is full of them."

"Somewhere *who* describes a dark gray cloud full of *what*?"
I ask him. He keeps reading:

> Those who have closed their minds to the possibility
> of life after death or who have led sordid, miserable
> existences will be completely baffled. (Smith, *The Book
> of James*)

"That's what we've got."

Now he's excited.

"We've got people completely baffled. They didn't know
what to expect. And that's what I try to tell the hitchhiker. You
didn't know what to expect, the Church has dropped the ball,
nobody's done what the Tibetans did twelve hundred years
ago—wasn't it twelve hundred years ago?"

"Wasn't *what* twelve hundred years ago?" He's rolling on
without me. "Wally." I stop him. Our eyes meet. "Who is the
hitchhiker?"

6

Who Is the Hitchhiker?

HITCHHIKER IS THE WORD WALLY USES FOR A SPIRIT who, for whatever reason, at the time of death becomes earthbound and instead of moving on attaches itself to a living human being.

I am suddenly full of questions. Attaches how? For what reason? What can happen? How can we become aware of it in ourselves and in others? What can be done about it? And what *did* the Tibetans do twelve hundred years ago?

Mark Greco was hit by a car. Teresa died in a fire. Carl's family perished from fever in three days. Likely, Hannah had been murdered. And after finding his trunk, Lonzo climbed to the top of a hill in the middle of a lightning storm.

Lorraine: *(Laughs) I returned from the tenth voyage . . . and I knew it was me last. And I took me trunk and I went looking for a room . . . and I found a room. Put me trunk in it . . . and I went out walking, if you can imagine— walking on dry land. And I walked up to the top of this . . . hill. And while I was walking, this thunderstorm came. And I got to the top of the hill and I stood there*

shouting: "You didn't get me, Ocean! You didn't get me,
you sea! I love you and I hate you and you didn't get me!"
And this bolt of lightning struck me from the heavens.
Wally: *Surprise, huh?*
Lorraine: *And me trunk went.*
Wally: *And you've been looking for that trunk ever since?*
Lorraine: *I watched it go.*
Wally: *Did you think it was here in Wisconsin?*
Lorraine: *I always knew where it was.*
Wally: *Is it in this house, Lonzo?*
Lorraine: *Yes!*
Wally: *Whereabouts?*
Lorraine: *I'm sitting on it! Can't you see?*

These were sudden and unexpected deaths. In such cases, the discarnate spirit often wanders confused, not knowing they are dead. They may hang out around the site of their death. Or they may follow their physical bodies to the hospital or to the funeral home or to the cemetery. Many never leave their cemetery plots. Others may be drawn to familiar surroundings or to a place that was important while they were physically alive, like Ezra Barren's long-gone house. Or like Lonzo, who couldn't leave the contents of his trunk. Ora hung out at a particular house because Teresa had sometimes been locked in an upstairs room there.

In each instance, Lorraine had been able to channel the entity and Wally was able to steer them toward the Light.

But, in the case of what Wally calls a hitchhiker, the disembodied spirit attaches itself to the aura of a person who is still alive. Perhaps a close relative or friend to whom they feel devoted and literally "cannot live without." Wives cling to husbands, husbands to wives. Dead mothers latch onto their own living children with sometimes the best of intentions to protect and give guidance, other times to meddle and interfere.

Or the hitchhiker may simply latch onto the first warm body passing by—a perfect stranger or unsuspecting bystander—and proceed to live vicariously through them, most often with no notion of what is going on. Sometimes for many years. Sometimes through consecutive lifetimes.

Says who?

In *The Book of James*, the spirit of a man who introduces himself as James Anderson dictates through Susy Smith's keyboard how he sees it from the other side.

At the moment of death we slip out of our physical bodies as we might an overcoat, says James, but we continue to exist in the form around which our physical bodies originally grew—our spirit body. There is no sudden change of personality and our surroundings appear as before. We are, in fact, exactly where we were, says James. And the essence of who we are continues.

The degree of confusion these conditions occasion is equal to the knowledge one has had in advance. If we expect death to be the ultimate blackout, end of everything, and instead, when it comes, nothing seems to have changed, we may continue to focus on the physical plane of people and things. Not realizing that we are dead, we may seek to satisfy our needs and appetites as we always have. It doesn't work.

Nobody talks to you. People act like you're not there. "If you roll over in bed and reach out for your wife and your hand goes through her," Wally tells me, "you're dead."

Without physical bodies, we no longer need shelter, food, or clothing, let alone sex, alcohol, or drugs. But if we die ignorant of our situation, if we don't know we are dead, or worse, have died under the influence of anger, alcohol, or drugs, our appetites remain, and we will blindly seek to satisfy them.

In *Return from Tomorrow*, George G. Ritchie tells the story of his own death in an army hospital at the age of twenty in 1943. If, as Raymond Moody says in the foreword to Ritchie's book, one defines death as "that state of the body from which no restoration of function is possible," then George Ritchie was not really dead. Yet, for nine minutes Ritchie's vital signs went flat, and what he saw and heard while "gone" changed his life.

He leaped up, turned around, and found the body of a young man in the bed where he had been. The body was his. Now out of his body, he began to float, then fly, "as if thought and motion had become the same thing," first over moonlit rural landscape, then down into an industrial city teeming with people. So many people, in fact, they seemed to be occupying the exact same space. Two men bore down on the same stretch of sidewalk and, amazed, Ritchie watched them walk right through each other.

Once aware that he had lost his ability to grasp things, or make contact or be seen or heard, Ritchie realized that his predicament was being shared by the frenzied glut of disembodied beings he saw milling about him, straining to be noticed by the living, snatching after cigarettes, begging forgiveness, yapping advice, and being thoroughly ignored.

"Disembodied beings, completely unsuspected by the living, hovered right on top of the physical things and people where their desires were focused," Ritchie writes.

A. E. Powell describes the astral plane as being a condition of nature rather than an actual location. In his classic book, *The Astral Body*, Powell states that "astral matter, being much finer than physical matter, interpenetrates it." Thus, a being living in the astral world may occupy the same space as a being living in the physical world, and the one will be entirely unconscious of the other and in no way impede their movements.

This situation of carnate and discarnate beings occupying the same space is described by paranormal investigator George W. Meek in *After We Die, What Then?* Meek says it is a condition peculiar to the lower zones of the astral level. Ritchie could see it because he was out of his body. Those of us in our bodies, still inhabiting the physical world, never know we are surrounded, in fact interpenetrated, by the spirit bodies of the ill-informed—for, according to Meek, to hang out down here on this level is to betray an ignorance of being dead.

Bereft of vision, hearing, taste, touch, and smell, and bewildered by the almost total darkness around them, the unknowing dead stumble on in a fog. Still ruled by their appetites, many latch onto the living and, ignorant of their condition, don't let go.

Moments later in his "death" experience, George G. Ritchie found himself in a dingy bar and grill crammed with sailors and civilians each "surrounded by a faint luminous glow almost like an electric field over the surface of their bodies. This luminosity moved as they moved like a second skin made out of pale, scarcely visible light." Again, the place was full of disembodied beings overlapping the living, grasping for shot glasses, pleading for beer, shouting out unseen, unheard. Ritchie noticed that, unlike the living, these dead had no light around them.

He watched a drunken sailor get off a stool, lose consciousness, and begin to fall. Before his body hit the floor, a crack opened up in the light cocoon around him and "quicker than I'd ever seen anyone move, one of the insubstantial beings disappeared inside the breach."

Twice more Ritchie watched the same scene repeat itself. A man passed out, a gap opened up in his aura, and one of the non-solid people seemed to vanish inside.

He concluded that this layer of light he saw around the living served as protection against the discarnate beings and that it was their loss of consciousness that rendered the living susceptible to being taken over.

Sixty years later, the existence of the human energy field is generally acknowledged now, even in the West. The energy principles known to Eastern yogis for centuries, and employed by Asian medicine for five thousand years, have finally found a grudging acceptance within Western medicine. Which is to say that technology has developed instrumentation capable of measuring it, which means that American insurance companies have finally agreed to begin to pay for it. "The invisible, which is the source of the visible," has once again—as with Elmer Green's biofeedback machine—been made visible. Thus are this culture's demands for veracity satisfied.

For decades, Kirlian photographs have made visible the human aura through interfacing ultra-low electrical current with the body's biological life field. Dr. Valerie Hunt's EMG machines display the electrical activity that exists around our chakras and throughout the human meridian system. Her video recordings document energy plumes of greatly varying sizes and shapes and colors routinely ballooning out from our own dense bodies—proof of Dolores Krieger's claim that "we don't end at our skin." Proof that human beings are, in fact, the energy fields that Martha Rogers theorized back in 1970, and that clairvoyants like Barbara Brennan work with every day.

Medical intuitive Carolyn Myss sees and reads these fields in her process of diagnosing diseases which, in collaboration with Dr. C. Norman Shealy, she has found to appear in our auric fields long before manifesting in our physical bodies.

This has all but become common knowledge now.

But in 1943, at the age of twenty, George G. Ritchie only knew what he saw. He didn't know what to call it—either the light around the living or his nine-minute floating fieldtrip to the other side. The term "Out of Body Experience" (OBE) would not surface until Robert Monroe published *Journeys Out of the Body* in 1971 to describe what started happening to him in 1958. In fact, it was George G. Ritchie's OBE itself that inspired Raymond Moody to start the research that led to his own best selling book, *Life After Life* (1975), from which came the term "Near Death Experience" (NDE).

Throughout history, unfortunates have been hung, drawn, quartered, drowned, burned at the stake, and otherwise made to pay for the alleged crime of demonic possession. The bulk of miracles attributed to Jesus in the Bible involve "the casting out of demons." According to Malachi Martin's *Hostage to the Devil* (1992 edition), the Catholic Church still performs between eight hundred and thirteen hundred exorcisms a year.

So, where do these "demons" come from? Where do they go? Are they truly demonic? Are these the hellspawn and incubi and succubi portrayed in Hollywood movies? The minions of Satan? Or just the souls of people who have died without knowing they are dead and in their ignorance, confusion, and fear have attached themselves to living human beings?

7

Teenage Druggies

"I'D WRITE THE BOOK FOR TEENAGE DRUGGIES," Wally told me. "And I'd start with George G. Ritchie's description of all these discarnate alcoholics waiting around for somebody to drink themselves into a stupor and pass out. I think kids that drink themselves into oblivion or drug themselves into oblivion should know the hazards that they're opening themselves up to and should understand that there's some nasty sons of bitches out there."

"It is our ignorance that renders us susceptible," I say out loud, and then write down.

"Or some people who may not be nasty," Wally went on, "but are desperately trying to kill themselves and may have succeeded with the last three or four people that they hitchhiked on, and I suggested this in *Take Charge*, that unexplained suicides could be just like this gal from Chicago that Carl Wickland talks about who took over Mrs. Wickland one day."

Take Charge: A Guide to Feeling Good is a book Wally wrote and published in 1987. In it he considers, among other things, the likelihood that suicides for which there seem to be no cause may in fact result from the kind of spirit attachment we are talking about. "This gal from Chicago" was the spirit of a woman who had killed herself by drinking carbolic acid but, as badly as she wanted to no longer be alive, had died completely ignorant of the nature of death. Still aware of her surroundings and what she assumed to be her body, she decided she had failed in her attempt to kill herself and so latched onto the next warm body she could find in order to kill herself again.

This time the body belonged to Anna Wickland, the psychic wife of psychiatrist Dr. Carl Wickland. His book *Thirty Years Among the Dead* (1924) is a treasure trove of verbatim dialogue between Dr. Wickland and the hitchhiking spirits he discovered to have attached themselves to patients in his psychiatric practice:

> If you are weak-willed and negative in your own personality, you may be led into crime, vice, or worse— suicide. Many have committed crimes or have taken their own lives because a voice . . . continually pressured them. . . .
>
> If in that state you go to a psychiatrist, he will treat you for psychosis. Many in institutions now are there because they hear voices or have strong compulsions to do things they do not really want to do. . . . If doctors would only realize that most of these persons are, in fact, being talked to by spirits, they could be cured. (Smith, *The Book of James*)

This is exactly what Dr. Carl Wickland realized. He first encountered the phenomenon while in medical school in Chicago when, after leaving the dissecting room, the spirit of the cadaver he'd been cutting on followed him home and started railing at him angrily through his psychic wife, Anna.

"Why are you trying to kill me? What do you mean by cutting me? Stop cutting me!" Anna yelled at Wickland as he came through the door.

Wickland tried to reason with the spirit, first placing Anna in a chair over the vigorous objection of the spirit not to touch him.

> To my answer that I had a right to touch my wife, the spirit entity retorted: "Your wife! What are you talking about! I am no woman. I'm a man!" (Wickland, *Thirty Years Among the Dead*)

Wickland counseled the entity as Wally later would—explaining to him that he had passed out of his physical body and was now in the body of Mrs. Wickland, that his spirit body was alive and here, but that his physical body was laid out dead on a table at the Dunham Medical College and would be of no further use to him.

When the truth of this finally dawned on the spirit, he agreed to leave but first begged Wickland for a chew of tobacco. Wickland refused. Well, then a pipe, said the spirit, "I'm dying for a smoke." Wickland could not imagine Anna sucking on a pipe, and again, told him no.

Back at the college, when Wickland reexamined the cadaver, he found the teeth of a life-long tobacco user.

■   ■   ■

Wally would write the book for teenage druggies and would try like hell to scare the pants off them.

"This gal from Chicago," for instance, literally knocked Anna Wickland out of her chair when she entered her aura on November 15, 1906. Through Anna, she kept saying, "Why didn't I take more carbolic acid? I want to die; I'm so tired of living."

Unable to see an electric light shining in her face, she complained of the darkness, saying over and over, "my poor son, my poor son." She said her name was Mary Rose and gave an address that later checked out. A Mary Rose had lived there with her son, but had been taken to the hospital a week before, where she had died. When asked if today's date was November 15, Mary Rose told Wickland, "No, that's next week."

Hospital records of the week before read: "Cook County Hospital, Chicago, Ill., Mary Rose, admitted November 7, 1906, died November 8, 1906, carbolic acid poisoning, no. 341106."

She'd been dead seven days and was still trying to kill herself.

> Like most suicides, she was in total ignorance of the indestructibility of life and the reality of the hereafter. When the real purpose of life, experience, and suffering had been made clear to her, she was overcome with repentance. (Wickland, *Thirty Years Among the Dead*)

Ritchie, too, reports seeing the spirits of people who had killed themselves only to realize that suicide is a temporary solution. Ritchie watched souls begging for forgiveness from loved ones in the physical world who could no longer see or hear them.

One young suicide followed an older man from room to room. "I'm sorry, Pa. I didn't know what it would do to Mama. I didn't understand." The old man carried a tray into a bedroom where an elderly woman lay grieving in bed. "I'm sorry, Mama," the young man said over and over.

Ritchie watched a teenage boy dog a teenage girl through the hallways of a high school. "I'm sorry, Nancy," he kept saying. "I'm sorry." And a middle-aged woman pleaded with an inconsolable gray-haired man who remained oblivious to her presence.

These are the lucky ones. These are the souls of suicides who realize what has happened. Those who don't, like Mary Rose, are left to wander alone in confusion and darkness or to attach themselves to one unsuspecting bystander after another.

"So, suicide," said Wally.

I go looking for a copy of *Thirty Years* among his books.

"I'd quote *The Book of James* about suicide and then I'd tell the reader who the real James is."

I turn around. The real James. The spirit who came to Susy Smith in 1967 calling himself James Anderson and proceeding to dictate that entire book through her in what—a week?

"William James," said Wally.

Harvard philosopher and scientist, author of *The Varieties of Religious Experience*, first president of the American Society for Psychical Research, brother of Henry James, born 1842, died 1910, William James had called for "radical empiricism."

Positivism ruled science at the time. It held that only that which could be observed by the senses—hence measured and repeated—could be the legitimate concern of scientific inquiry.

But William James was willing to explore everything and insisted that the range of scientific investigation be expanded to include all human experience—from the so-called objective to the so-called subjective, from the visible into invisible realms.

"How widely he meant this to be applied is indicated by the fact that he was involved for twenty-five years with exploration of psychic phenomena, spiritism, and religious experience. He was not convinced of the conclusion of enthusiasts in these areas, but he insisted that the experiences are appropriate data for a complete science." (From Willis Harman's introduction to Irene Hickman's *Remote Depossession*.)

Spiritism is the belief that the living can communicate with the dead. Spiritualism as a religious movement grew from mesmerism, which got started in France in the 1830s. Soon, Ouija boards, séances, and psychic circles became the rage in America as well. Theosophy became a movement. Talking to the dead through mediums became something certain people believed in, something certain people did.

If William James himself was "not convinced of the conclusions of enthusiasts in these areas," Dr. Carl and Anna Wickland certainly were.

Daily, the doctor was seeing how the faddish use of the "supposedly innocent" Ouija board was throwing open doors to every kind of spirit out there. "There are many passing from Earth life who . . . find themselves in somebody's magnetic aura and cannot get out, and they obsess that person," he wrote.

Wickland believed that many murders and holdups were being committed by spirits, and was soon convinced that the majority of patients in his practice were not suffering psychosis or mental aberrations at all, but were literally possessed by earthbound entities who, "owing to a lack of education concerning the spiritual side of their natures, continued to remain in earthly haunts."

Wickland blamed the Church for this lack of education, saying, "Jesus taught the existence of spirits and the spirit world," but "the Church limits itself to faith alone, and does not desire to add the required knowledge regarding the natural continuation of the spirit after death."

Unschooled by the Church and ignorant of their condition, these hitchhikers become "the cause of untold mischief and misery, often producing invalidism, immorality, crime, and seeming insanity."

To the dual end of relieving the torment and confusion of both his patients and the spirits who attached to them,

Wickland built what he called the "Wimhurst" machine. A static electricity generator, it contained fourteen thirty-inch-diameter glass discs, "all active," he wrote, "giving a powerful current." While not strong enough to cause physical harm to his patient, the jolt sufficed to dislodge the earthbound entity from the patient's aura and to send it leaping into the body of his wife. There he could talk to the entity, explain the situation, and encourage them to get on with their spiritual development.

"My God and Stars in Heaven, how it hit me!" one complained. "Lightning played around my head until I didn't know where I was."

"What in the world did you put all those needles in me for?"

"I won't stay here. I'm going. You put fire on my back."

"You felt the electricity I gave to a patient," Wickland told them.

Spirit: *No, do not touch me! I don't want your hands on me! I am afraid of that fire! (Stamping feet.)*

Wickland: *Did you always have bad manners?*

Spirit: *Why did you take me away from where I was? I have no place to go . . . . I want to be with that little girl. She belongs to me.*

Wickland: *She does not belong to you. She is no relation of yours. What right do you have to bother that little girl?*

Spirit: *(Crying) I want her!*

Wickland: *You will not bother that little girl any more.*

Spirit: *You let go my hands.*

Wickland: *I'm not holding your hands. I am holding my wife's hands.*

Spirit: *I don't like you.*

Wickland: *You are using my wife's body, but only for a*

*short time. You are an ignorant earthbound spirit and
have been hovering around that little girl and have
now been taken away from her.* (Wickland, *Thirty
Years Among the Dead*)

Wickland worked like this for many years, always with Anna,
usually in the context of a psychic circle, which he says
included the aid of intelligent spirits and higher beings whose
intention it is to help lost souls make their way to the Light.

Inspiration for the Wimhurst had come from the writings
of John Wesley, founder of the Methodist Church. Wesley had
run clinics in London 140 years before, where he'd used static
electricity to treat lunacy, epilepsy, headaches, paralysis, and
convulsions. Though inspired by Wesley, Wickland designed
his machine to the specifications of the same intelligent spirits
who gathered for the circles where he used the Wimhurst until
Anna's death in 1937, at which time Wickland retired.

"It seems likely that today's still-controversial use of elec-
troshock, or electroconvulsive therapy, for the treatment of acute
depression may prove effective, when it does, for the unacknowl-
edged reason that it drives possessing earthbound spirits out of
the magnetic aura of the subjects being shocked," is a note I
wrote to myself. I will insert it here and take a break. A breather.
Push back from the table. Put my feet up. Chill.

■   ■   ■

Okay.

What *is* this "spiritual development" Wickland steers his
disembodied beings toward?

What is life's so-called "higher meaning" he seems so certain of?

What is "the truth of the hereafter"?

"The real purpose to life"?

Like Wickland, Wally counsels lost souls to turn away from him and to call out to loved ones, to get on with their business, to move on to the Light.

What is our business?

And what is "the Light"?

William James, as always, seems certain: "Man lives his life on earth . . . to individualize himself and establish his identity and character."

> The Soul or consciousness of each baby born on the various inhabited planets of the universe comes from Divine Consciousness . . . and goes through its life cycle learning what it can from the experiences it encounters, dies to the physical body and emerges as a spirit in whatever stage of personal character development it has attained up to that time. (Smith, *The Book of James*)

So, for James, our souls are here for the first time ever, for one lifetime, for the purpose of establishing an identity which, by its own efforts at spiritual development, may eventually achieve a state of higher being.

But what does that mean, exactly?

Wally puts it this way:

"The business of life is to raise your vibrations through thought, word, and deed. So that you reduce your mass and increase your frequency. Everything is made of light, and light has two characteristics, the product of which is a constant— the speed of light. The two characteristics are wavelength and frequency. As you approach love and compassion in thought, word, and deed, your vibrations increase and your mass goes down. Your energy is the same, but it's in a different form. E equals mc squared. See the algebra of it?"

E equals mc squared. We are here to reduce our mass and to raise our vibrations. I do see the algebra of that, yes. And it reminds me of something from Jin Shin Jyutsu, which I followed Ruth into—not the practice of it (she became a practitioner), but the study of it (I took the workshop).

Jin Shin Jyutsu is the five-thousand-year-old Japanese art of acupressure. One of its principles is that matter and spirit exist at opposite ends of the same continuum. Thus, they differ only in degree. In Jin Shin, spirit is understood to be the finest form of matter. Matter is understood to be the densest form of spirit.

Suddenly, I'm thinking of Drunvalo Melchizedek, who first leaped off the shelf at me in the Green Apple Bookstore on Clement in San Francisco. The book was *Nothing in This Book Is True but It's Exactly How Things Are.* It wasn't by him. The book is about him. Since then, Drunvalo himself has written books where he describes, among many mysteries, the difference between dimensional worlds as being a condition of the frequency at which matter vibrates within these worlds.

As do Sufis and theoretical physicists, Drunvalo believes that everything in the universe vibrates. Hence, everything in the universe can be described by its wavelength, or "the distance from any point on the sine wave curve to the point where the entire curve starts over."

According to Drunvalo, the wavelength of the third-dimensional physical world we live in is 7.23 centimeters. As you go up into higher dimensional levels, the wavelengths get shorter and the energy gets higher. As you go down, wavelengths lengthen and energy weakens. Matter grows more dense.

"It's like a television or radio set," he says. "When you turn the dial, you pick up a different wavelength, and you get a different image on your TV screen. It's exactly the same for dimensional levels." (Melchizedek, *The Ancient Secret of the Flower of Life*, vol. 1)

So, the purpose of life is to change channels, right?

Abruptly, Elmer Green pops into my head. Something he said about a human being having not one, but two souls—an immortal SOUL, which he capitalizes and calls our True Self, and a mortal soul he calls the astral body, what we think of as "ourselves." This lowercase soul is the conscious and subconscious alloy of two kinds of subtle matter—emotion and thought—which when combined with the denser physical substance, makes up the personality.

> After the personality's loss of its physical body at death, its still-surviving self, the soul, finds itself in a domain called, in Tibet, the after-death bardo . . . .This bardo consists of many gradations of emotional and mental substance into which the soul "rises" like a balloon until it reaches that level in the Earth's emotional-mental atmosphere which corresponds with the density or subtlety of its feelings and thoughts . . . during its just-completed life on earth. (Green, *The Ozawkie Book of the Dead*)

This magnetic attraction of sympathetic thoughts and feelings is exactly how Robert Monroe describes the soul's movement through nonphysical realms after leaving the body at death.

Monroe says that the soul moves through what he calls Belief System Territories and can be attracted to and literally pulled off into a concentration of similar beliefs. He conjures up the image of a Celestial Interstate—an Eisenhower

Expressway of motoring souls that are suddenly swept off down an exit ramp into the vibrational hamlet to which they are attuned.

It is in this way that Lutherans find themselves with Lutherans, Catholics resonate with Catholics, racists get stuck with racists, and thieves with thieves.

Monroe's knowledge about how this works is based on more than thirty years experience with out-of-body travel.

A successful businessman who owned radio stations and worked on Madison Avenue, Monroe had neither knowledge of nor interest in paranormal events until one night in 1958, when he suddenly found himself floating out of his body, bumping gently against the ceiling of his bedroom. Below him lay his sleeping wife and his own physical body, which sounds like countless accounts of Near Death Experiences reported since. But this was 1958. Raymond Moody had yet to write *Life After Life*. And Monroe hadn't died. And he wasn't asleep, wasn't dreaming. He was vibrating like crazy he knew not why, but he was wide awake. And gripped with fear. Was he losing his mind? Did he have a brain tumor? Who could he ask? He didn't even tell his wife.

"Monroe went to his friend, a psychologist, and also I think his family doctor, and the psychologist said, 'No, I don't think you're crazy. Take notes,'" Wally told me.

Take notes.

"'Just keep track of the weather and the barometric pressure and everything that's going on.' And this is what he did.

"His medical doctor said, 'I vaguely remember in med school we had some guys from India and they talked about soul travel.' So, I think this quieted him down as far as being crazy, and started him on a scientific exploration of whatever this was."

Monroe took notes. He paid close attention to exactly how it happened when it happened again, and it continued to happen every other day or so for weeks.

Eventually, he learned how to bring on the condition. Later, he learned how to control and direct it. He started leaving his body deliberately to visit friends, sometimes hundreds of miles away, and then return to his body, later verifying that, yes, they had been walking their retriever in the moonlight at that moment in a yellow rain slicker. No, they had not seen him. But he had seen them.

Monroe soon found himself traveling outside physical dimensions, exploring "the nonphysical energy field that permeates time-space, including our Earth Life System, but is not a part of current human scientific knowledge and study."

This sounds to me like the after-death bardo described by Elmer Green, the same astral landscape where Mark Greco and Ezra Barrens and Hannah and Lonzo got stuck. Monroe began conducting spirit retrievals "out there," first of individual human souls trapped in their ignorance of being dead, and later, large-scale rescue missions involving masses of entities killed in earthquakes, floods, and other disasters who were frozen in the moment of their sudden deaths.

Monroe's curiosity had overwhelmed his fears. He established the Monroe Institute in the rolling folds of the Shenandoah Valley and continued to do research, determined that what he believed would be based on direct experience rather than taken on faith. He had discovered reality to be more than it appears to be. Now he began to translate other Unknowns into Knowns. For instance:

Known: We are more than our physical bodies.

Known: There is no such thing as death.

Known: Our consciousness survives so-called death. That's

whether we like it or not, in fact. Regardless of what we do on Earth, our consciousness survives.

Known: Where we go when our soul leaves our body depends in large part on *what we believe*. That is, at what frequency our thoughts vibrate; literally, depending on *the resonance of our beliefs*.

Journeys Out of the Body came out in 1971. Monroe's account of traveling through the uncharted terrain of alternative realities and mind-consciousness found ready readership at a time when altered states were becoming a lifestyle choice for a turned-on generation. Monroe found himself on the bookshelf next to Carlos Castenada and John C. Lilly and Timothy Leary and Ram Dass.

■   ■   ■

Bardo.

The word is Tibetan for "between-state." Tibetan Buddhists believe that the bardo is a stretch of hostile territory every soul must cross between death and rebirth.

Tibetan Buddhists believe in reincarnation.

William James believes our individual consciousness survives death but does not reincarnate. Elmer Green believes that our individual consciousness survives death, but does not survive the absorption by our uppercase SOUL, which then creates a new personality that *does* reincarnate.

Tibetan Buddhists believe that our consciousness survives death to go on living lifetime after lifetime, but that at every physical death we run the very real risk of losing human consciousness and devolving into lower animal realms. If we're not careful, we can come back as a monkey, dog, or donkey. The responsibility is entirely our own.

What introduces an element of urgency into the matter is that they also believe that the soul has only forty-nine Earth days to successfully make its trip across the bardo and to reincarnate into the body of a human.

In Tibet, the book we call *The Tibetan Book of the Dead* is known as the *Bardo Thodol,* or *The Great Book of Natural Liberation Through Understanding in the Between* and was written by Padme Sambava in the eighth or ninth century.

This is what the Tibetans did twelve hundred years ago.

They wrote a guidebook. And they began the ritual practice of reading out loud to their newly departed from this detailed description of what to expect and how to safely make the trip.

The book is a travel guide through a perilous minefield. I mean, *mind* field. Because "everything we experience on the bardos is a reflection of our own mental machinations." (H. Smith, introduction to *The Tibetan Book of the Dead,* Robert A. Thurman, trans.) Whatever flesh-eating demons or monsters may appear to block our path, are not real. They are mental projections of the doubts, fears, expectations, and beliefs that our soul has held in its just-lived lifetime.

Nothing is real. All is thought. In fact, The Clear Light of the Void, if and when it appears, is finally understood to be nothing less than our own immortal essence. The belief is that our recognition of this truth and our sought-for liberation are simultaneous.

■   ■   ■

Wally stops me.

"You've inserted some pretty esoteric stuff that takes us off the nitty-gritty of 'Do you really want to turn your body over to a dead son of a bitch?'"

He's right. The fine points here will likely be lost on our teenage druggie, whose intention, after all, is not so much to raise his consciousness as to lose it entirely.

"We're talking about American teenagers and some of their hazards, their ignorance," he said. "The Church hasn't taught them, and school hasn't taught them, mental health class hasn't taught them. Fact, they'd probably fire the mental health teacher that brought it up."

People who don't know they're dead can be hazardous to teenagers who don't know what they're doing.

"At this stage in their life, where they're experimenting, looking for sensations of all kinds, getting them wherever they can, they open up their auras. They're invincible they think.

"But, if you don't get wise to a hitchhiker, you can be led a lot of different places, with a lot of different urges or addictions. And, if you've got hitchhikers on you, this can slow you down from where you're headed. Or, do you know where you're headed? Are you just here to enjoy yourself? To get through the pain? Just to get it over with? You didn't ask to be born, right?

"Let me get back to the Belief System," Wally said.

"We started out with two beliefs that I think are crucial: Is the universe friendly or unfriendly? That sends you on two very divergent paths.

"And what happens at death? What you believe there also sends you on two very divergent paths. One is, 'It's a jungle out there. This is a dog-eat-dog universe and you don't do unto others the way you want them to do unto you. You do unto others *before* they can do it to you. You only go around once in life, so grab all the gusto you can get.' This is a beer commercial! That *creates a level of vibration, an attractor field, that thinks on that level.*"

And attracts your life.

"The other belief would be: This is one of my many lifetimes and I'm here to learn to be more loving and compassionate. And to raise my vibrations through thought, word, and deed.

"We just started talking about these people who are dead and don't know they are dead, and now you're walking right into it. It's like you're opening up the bedroom door with a Ouija board, only worse. You've gone out to where they've concentrated. A dead, earthbound alcoholic is not going to hang out in the cemetery. He's going to hang out in a bar."

Or a nightclub. Or a crack house. Or a rave.

"So, hey, before you shoot up, you who are so proud of your independence, think about this. You want to be in control, right? You're in charge of your life? Not taking orders from anybody? And now you're going to go out and get smashed and turn your body and your mind and your emotions and your money over to some nasty discarnate addict that you don't even know—who is DEAD!—who has no right to your body, and wants to use it for his benefit and spend your money for his kicks? You really want to be *independent*? Or do you want to be a slave to some dead son of a bitch that doesn't even know he's dead? Come on, kid, shape up!"

■　　　■　　　■

In a perfect world, Wally's teenage druggie might be persuaded to change his behavior. But, what if she's not? What if our teenage druggie finally doesn't give a rip? Who should?

Anyone who cares about the teenage druggie. Anyone who may be trying to develop compassion and to raise their vibrations through thought, word, and deed. Anyone who is interested in helping to thin out that dark gray cloud William James says encircles our planet and is full of the chattering, ignorant spirits of people who are dead and do not know it.

Certainly, anyone who may suspect that a friend or a loved one might be attached by an earthbound spirit.

And, what if *you* are attached?

How would you know?

Dr. Edith Fiore presents a list of symptoms in *The Unquiet Dead* (1988). She says the most common signs of spirit possession include:

- fatigue
- mood swings
- hearing voices
- abuse of drugs and alcohol
- impulsive behavior
- poor concentration
- memory problems
- sudden onset of anxiety or depression
- sudden onset of physical problems with no obvious cause.

Not everyone who finds herself on this list is possessed by an earthbound spirit. Edith Fiore calls these "signs." But, physical conditions like exhaustion, depression, negative thinking, and substance abuse, can actually *attract* attachment. *Can be both symptomatic and causal.*

So, the answer to the next question—Who is at risk?— must begin with anyone presenting with symptoms listed above, and draw a thick dark line under "abuse of drugs and alcohol." Those who work in or hang out in bars, saloons, or nightclubs, where alcohol and/or drugs are used and where people routinely lose consciousness, are at risk. People who work around the dead, sick, and dying—nurses, orderlies, paramedics, ambulance drivers, firemen, policemen, and soldiers—are at risk. People who visit and/or stay overnight in hospitals. Patients who go under anesthesia. Those who undergo surgery, blood transfusions, and organ transplants. Researchers now suggest that the receiver of a donated organ may, in effect, be donating their body to an unknown entity or entities attached to the organ they receive.

Often, hospice workers and home healthcare providers develop close and loving relationships with people who are dying. Many times, the dying do not want to let go, and so hang on. They may go home with their caring friends and neither one's the wiser.

Fact is, everyone is at risk. "I doubt if you could walk through a mall without picking one up," said Wally.

8

Walking Through the Mall

DR. EDITH FIORE CAME TO POSSESSION through hypnosis. A licensed clinical psychologist, she began using hypnotic trance with her clients as the fastest way into the subconscious mind, where our memories are stored. She began tapping into early childhood memories and birth experiences, including things said at the time of delivery. Some of her clients retrieved lost memories of the intrauterine period between conception and birth. One case resolved itself with the client's memory of her own attempted abortion.

Then one day in response to her standard trance instruction to "regress to the event responsible for the problem," her client found himself as a Catholic priest in the seventeenth century. Fiore says she knew nothing about past lives and did not believe in reincarnation. Nevertheless, she treated the client as if his condition was real, and his symptoms disappeared.

In following weeks, more clients regressed to former lives, and when Fiore treated the condition as fact not fantasy, their symptoms also disappeared. Her first book, *You Have Been Here Before* (1978), is her account of treating more than a thousand people in over twenty thousand hypnotic regressions for problems stemming from past lives.

When, in these early years, she found clients slipping into other personalities while in hypnotic trance, and conditions didn't fit the therapeutic framework for past lives, Fiore began by assuming they may be manifesting multiple personalities, but more and more, these conditions seemed to point to something else.

She couldn't make sense of the sheer numbers of personalities that seemed to inhabit some people, or of the way some personalities appeared to come and go without showing up again, or how multiple regressions sometimes overlapped in time. These cases seemed to call for a different model. Above all, her clients weren't responding to treatment for multiple personality. Their behaviors didn't change.

Having started to read metaphysical texts, including *The Tibetan Book of the Dead*, Fiore began listening to her clients as if discarnate spirits might be causing their problems. She began to hear her clients in a different way when they said things like, "My husband says to me I'm two completely different people," "When I drink, I'm not myself," or "I hear a voice say to me 'You'll never stay on that diet.'"

Fiore didn't believe in the reality of spirit possession any more than she believed in past lives, but when she acted as if her clients were possessed and began performing depossessions on them, their symptoms disappeared and did not come back.

In *The Unquiet Dead* (1988), Fiore writes that her "practice now consists of using hypnosis to get to the cause of the problem, whether it is from a repressed memory of an event in this lifetime, past lives, or the presence of one or more possessing entities."

Fiore uses possession as a working hypothesis. When possession is what appears to be happening, she proceeds as if it is. Like Wally, she views the possessing entity as her true client. Like Wally, she seeks to relieve their suffering by affecting their release from the earth plane so that they may get on with the business of spiritual evolution.

But, whereas Wally's access to spirits comes through Lorraine's ability as a medium to step aside and willingly allow an entity to possess her, Fiore uses hypnotic trance to connect through the subconscious mind of her client to the earthbound spirit who is using them as an "unwilling medium" without their knowledge or consent.

■   ■   ■

About the time I imagine Edith Fiore was handing in her manuscript for the publication of *The Unquiet Dead*, my aunt Ruth was diagnosed with cancer.

A lot had happened in the thirteen years since Wally'd introduced the two of us to biofeedback in that Omaha motel room. He and Ardis had spent the next six years working with Vic and Lorraine, though since 1981 they had seen little of them. Vic had taken up with a chain-smoking social worker and moved with her to Franklin, Tennessee.

Without Vic and Lorraine, Wally had pretty much retired from counseling spirits.

Vic married the social worker and soon got very sick. Ten years his junior, his new wife told her friends, "Well, I married him for better or worse, but not this."

She had a really snowy, off-the-antenna recording of the movie *E.T.*, Wally told me, and she put that on and put Vic in his wheelchair in front of the TV set and drove off with a girl-friend the one time Wally came to visit.

Vic was inarticulate and wheelchair-bound. "He could say a couple three words if you got him pissed off enough, but that's the only way you could get him to talk," Wally told me.

Finally, Vic's new wife refused to take care of him at all. So, Lorraine came down and brought Vic back to the farmhouse she was living in in Iowa. There Lorraine took care of Vic until he died.

Meanwhile, Ruth had left Detroit to become Director of Graduate Nursing at Rutgers University in Newark, New Jersey. Her then-housemate and long-time companion, Margie, had moved with her from Michigan and was now helping take care of Ruth's ninety-something-year-old mother (my grandma), who had moved in with them. But Margie had just recently come out of remission, and there was trouble ahead.

I was working on Ruth's house in Metuchen—building walls, hanging doors, putting in a backyard deck—and was able to spend time with Grandma as she "sorted out her life." Off and on, I would find her talking to Grandpa, who'd been dead forty years. Or, she would ask about the people upstairs. There are no people upstairs, I would tell her. This is a one-story house. "Then what about the couple with the baby?"

My memory of Ruth at this time was that these episodes with Grandma seemed for her to point not so much to the "other side," as they did for me, as to the possibility of over-medication. And maybe she was right. Maybe not.

I do know that taking care of Grandma was becoming too much for Margie. And I remember seeing Ruth come home from work completely frazzled, white knuckles tight around her briefcase handle, shoulders up around her ears. She was finding academic life at Rutgers stressful. Personalities didn't jibe. World views collided. Eventually, backstabbing was introduced. Ruth didn't like it.

Then Grandma fell and broke her pelvic bone. Ruth flew with her to Portland, where Grandma moved in with Wally and Ardis for the final eighteen months of her life. During that next year and a half, Margie grew sick and died. After that, Ruth decided to resign her job and take early retirement. Only after she, too, had moved to Portland did Ruth become aware of the cancer.

"On the Holmes and Ray Stress Indicator I was out of this world," Ruth told me. "Mom dying in February and Margie in April and the job situation, relocating, you name it."

1987. Thirty-five out of thirty-seven lymph nodes tested positive. Her oncologist pushed for immediate surgery followed by aggressive chemotherapy and radiation treatments, and Ruth said wait.

"Cancer is an immuno-suppressive disorder," she told me. "The treatments they were offering me suppressed the immune system. To deliberately do something that would suppress the immune system when you're already about to succumb to an immuno-suppressive disorder makes no kind of sense." Her conviction was based on Martha Rogers and the fact that, including herself, she'd been close to six women who'd been diagnosed with cancer and had so far buried four.

The other woman still standing was Wally's wife. Ardis had refused chemotherapy and radiation following her surgery in 1974. She had read Dr. Crile's book, *What Every Woman Should Know About Breast Cancer*, "and he just abhorred this massive surgery they did to remove the whole breast," Ardis said. Then she and Wally discovered *Getting Well Again*, a book by O. Carl Simonton, a medical doctor and Air Force major who had previously been a salesman whose success he attributed to Napoleon Hill's classic book, *Think And Grow Rich*. Simonton's techniques were based on Positive Prosperity Visualization.

So, after surgery, "I employed his tactics of visualizing at the time PacMan, the TV game? Just visualizing PacMan eating up all those cancer cells," said Ardis. She combined this with biofeedback and her body has been cancer-free for more than thirty years.

After Ruth's biopsy but before deciding what to do, Wally took her to a Bernie Siegel workshop in Seattle that was sponsored by the American Holistic Medical Association. Wally delivered a hug to Siegel, author of *Love, Medicine and Miracles*, from their mutual friend, Elisabeth Kubler-Ross, "and Ruth was surrounded with that kind of people," Wally said.

"The message I got from Siegel," Ruth told me, "was that the people who were surviving were the people who were taking control of their lives, not the people who were submissively following whatever their medical advisors told them to do."

Martha Rogers had talked about the fact that cancer patients were being programmed to expect to die and programmed to accept the chemo/radiation regimen largely because that's all that Western medicine had to offer, and because that's what insurance companies were willing to pay for, and, as Ruth's new housemate and long-time friend, Laurel, liked to put it: "If all you've got is a hammer, everything looks like a nail."

"The missing link in Western medicine is their total ignorance of energy," Ruth told me. "And of us as energetic beings. Western medicine is based on the study of cadavers, so it's strong in anatomy. The Chinese were never allowed to do autopsies, so they had to study the living being."

About this time, Wally referred Ruth to a Chinese acupuncturist he had seen on a local TV show. The man's work was having a positive effect on immune enhancement. So, Ruth began getting treatments from this man.

Next, she and Wally went to Topeka for a conference on the effects of megadoses of Vitamin C on terminal cancer, "which, as far as the oncologist was concerned," Ruth said, "I had terminal metastatic CA, no question in his mind." Ruth still had questions in her mind, if not about the need for surgery, about how she was going to live her post-op life in harmony with what she somehow sensed her body knew it needed. How could she tune into what her body knew?

It was at the conference in Topeka that Ruth discovered Healing Touch and, more importantly, the pendulum.

Healing Touch is an energy-based therapeutic approach to healing that borrows from Dora Kunz and Dolores Krieger's Therapeutic Touch. TT itself borrows from psychic healing, the ancient art of the laying on of hands, and principles set forth by Martha Rogers.

The operating assumption is that, in addition to a physical body, we have (and literally are) also a subtle energy body comprised of many interpenetrating fields (the aura) connected by chakras. These invisible disk-like vortexes called chakras connect with the invisible meridian pathways along which moves the subtle energy called prana, chi, ki, life force. Whatever word is used to describe it, what is being described is the soul that goes on living after our physical body dies. Our energetic essence.

Health here is understood to be physical, emotional, mental, and spiritual harmony or balance within this system. Balance is achieved through an interaction of energies, an allowing of universal life force to move through both healer and healee.

The principal diagnostic tool used for assessment is the pendulum. This can be a small cut crystal or tear-shaped stone on a short chain, or even a paperclip tied to a length of dental floss.

Ruth watched the workshop facilitator use her pendulum to check the chakras of a volunteer stretched out on the massage table. Holding her pendulum a few inches above the woman's body, the facilitator moved along her midline from one chakra to the next. Ruth could see it move—sometimes clockwise, sometimes counterclockwise, maybe back and forth, sometimes describing an ellipse, sometimes stopping altogether—depending on the quality of energy flowing in and out of the body at each chakra point. Ruth tried it.

Rendering visible the otherwise invisible subtle energy within the body's fields, the pendulum functions as a feedback loop. ("Without feedback, nothing can be learned," said Elmer Green.) The pendulum gives the healer a glimpse of what a medical intuitive can see in a person's aura. For Ruth it also seemed to connect somehow with the knowledge she intuited that the body has about itself.

Before leaving the convention, Ruth signed up for Level 1 of Healing Touch in Raleigh. And she bought herself a pendulum.

By the time she and Wally got back to Portland, she had made her decision. She would say yes to the surgery (which was not immuno-suppressive) and no to the chemo/radiation, thinking that, "if I got rid of the bulk of it, I could then fight the rest of it naturally." She would choose to do only those things purported to enhance immune function.

Her oncologist told her that her choice was suicidal. Ruth would not survive. If she refused to do what he told her to do, she would be dead in two years, he told her. That was 1987.

■   ■   ■

Edith Fiore gave a lecture on past life regression to a local Society of Clinical Hypnosis in southern California in 1980. William Baldwin, a dentist who'd been studying hypnosis as an adjunct to dentistry, was sitting in the audience. The experience changed his life.

Baldwin went on to train with Fiore and with Dr. Morris Netherton (*Past Lives Therapy*, 1978), became certified in the Netherton Method of Past-Life Therapy, and started seeing patients. Soon, he got his Ph.D. in clinical psychology and went on to literally "write the book" on the hypnotherapeutic treatment of possession by earthbound spirits. Baldwin's *Spirit Releasement Therapy* (1992) is *the* technique manual on the subject. He and Edith Fiore became the acknowledged experts in the field.

Add to their research and clinical experience the work of Carl Wickland, Ralph Allison, Adam Crabtree, Irene Hickman, Hans Naegeli-Osjord, Eugene Maurey, Samuel Sagan, and Louise Ireland-Frey, and you have pretty much what Wally has in his library on the topic.

I pulled a book off Wally's shelf. It fell open to a note card. Scribbled on the card was: "Recent research has shown us that being dead is so much like being alive that many people die without realizing their condition." I turned to Wally. "That's a quote from Baldwin, right?"

"I don't know where it came from," Wally said, which is frequently the case. "Some of what I think is mine often came from somewhere else, just passed through me. If I thought it was important, I saved it. And after I save it, then I rediscover it and think it's mine. I made it mine by thinking it was important."

Wally is a synthesizer, an eclectic thinker, a connector of theories and facts. "I just keep bumping into stuff that feels significant," he tells me. He may not remember where it all comes from, but he has spent his adult life seeing how it fits into what he calls the Cosmic Jigsaw Puzzle and sharing with others what he's found. He's not an academic, not a scholar. He is a counselor and a teacher and a student, always has been.

It's funny. Some of the family have little patience with Wally. At least one (by marriage) has alleged that what he and Ruth are doing is the work of the Devil. Of course, the family is large and accommodates a wide variety of viewpoints. Others simply say it is impossible to have a conversation with him. I say that's only true if you're not interested at all in what so totally consumes him, and I always have been. Interested in what he knows, in what he's reading, what he's thinking, what he's writing, where he's going with his theories, what is linking up with what. He walks the mall of ideas and theories and books.

Earlier, I jumped from William James to Elmer Green to Drunvalo Melchizedick to Bob Monroe to *The Book of the Dead* to Raymond Moody, and back to Elmer Green. Wally would call this a serious case of "cerebral corn popping." This is his process, and, once started, he is hard to stop. I've never tried to stop him. In fact, I move a bit the same way.

Six foot one, lanky, Wally wears slim-cut, sky blue jeans with a waist-length matching jacket from Penney's, white crosstrainers, and a baseball cap, as if this were a uniform. The badge on his cap says "Retired Air Force." He is a major. Having flown B-25s during World War II, he was recalled for Korea in 1951 and spent the next eight years in the Strategic Air Command (SAC) as a pilot and Aircraft Commander of B-29s and B-47s.

Wally's center of gravity seems to rest behind the eyes, at his sixth chakra, the brow chakra. Wally tends to move tilted slightly forward as if leaning into what is coming next, as if being pulled by an invisible thread tied to his pineal gland. Science long considered the pineal gland to be useless. We now consider it the source of inner light, the maker of melatonin, seat of seeing and insight.

But, like I say, he has no small talk. Wally doesn't chat.

9

As If

There may be no such thing as life after death.
—RAYMOND A. MOODY, JR.

NO ONE LIVING KNOWS EXACTLY WHAT DEATH IS. No one knows for sure where we go or if we do, and if we do, what happens when we get there. Even Raymond Moody, who introduced the concept of Near Death Experience into the cultural consciousness with *Life After Life* in 1975, says he never meant to present his work as proof of the existence of life after death.

> The media did that. And my publishers did that, with the way they edited and marketed the book. I simply meant to report the experiences of people who were "near death." I never assumed myself to be reporting the experiences of people *after* death, nor have I ever reached the conclusion that because people were having certain kinds of experiences when they were near to death, an ongoing "life" after death had now been proven beyond question. The purpose of my first book, in fact, was to *raise* the question, not to *answer* it. (Moody, *The Last Laugh*)

As with Fiore and Baldwin, researchers and therapists in the field of spirit releasement do not claim to know exactly what happens. They keep the question open and proceed *as if* certain things are true, because when they do so, their clients' symptoms seem to disappear.

> I discovered that when the possession experience was treated as if it were exactly what it appeared to be—invasion and control of the client by another human spirit—the condition could almost always be cleared up. Success did not depend upon my conviction or my client's that the experience corresponded to a metaphysical reality; it was only necessary for us to accept the experience itself as valid and worthy of serious attention. (Crabtree, *Multiple Man*)

And so, researchers and therapists in the field proceed as if:

- We are more than our physical bodies.
- We are a body within a mind, not a mind within a body.
- Consciousness exists separate from the body.
- Survival of consciousness beyond physical death is a reality.
- Communication with those who have left the physical body is possible.
- The invasion and control of a living being by another human spirit . . . happens.

Still, no one knows exactly what death is.

An exception to this may be Mark Macy and his work with Instrumental Transcommunication (ITC). Macy claims to communicate directly with the dead. In his book, *Conversations Beyond the Light: Communication with Departed Friends and Colleagues by Electronic Means* (1995), he and Dr. Pat Kubis describe a group of discarnate scientists on the other side who are dedicated to communicating directly with the living by sending words and pictures through our tape recorders, telephones, radios, TVs, computers, and fax machines.

Unlike with psychic mediums or automatic writing, the messages ITC receives are not filtered through the brain, mind, or voice box of a living human being, but come directly from the dead "through electronic means."

According to Macy, the spirit group called Timestream is in frequent contact with colleagues in laboratories all over the world. The group is headed by a small team of spirit scientists that includes Thomas Edison, Marie Curie, Wernher von Braun, Albert Einstein, and a Latvian psychologist named Konstantin Raudive, whose book, *Breakthrough* (1971), rocked the scientific community while he was still alive.

Using an ordinary reel-to-reel tape recorder, Raudive sat alone in his lab and asked questions of departed friends and loved ones. He let his tape recorder run on for hours at a time, and while he monitored the tape, the dead began to speak.

According to Raudive, communication is telepathic on the astral plane. The dead neither have nor need larynxes to communicate with each other. But, in order to talk to those alive on Earth, these spirits have had to learn to modulate sound waves with their thoughts to create voice patterns. They instructed Raudive to tune his radio to the "white noise" static between stations. They then used these vibrations to create words he could hear and record on tape.

Raudive collected over seventy-five thousand short, faint spirit voices on tape this way, documenting over fifteen thousand of them while he was alive. Now dead, he works with other scientists of Timestream, whose "electronic bridge" of video and sound transmission techniques have become so advanced that the second biggest obstacle to communicating with us now is the primitive state of our own equipment.

Having gone beyond television transmissions, they now access the hard drives of computers on Earth and leave detailed, computer-scanned images as well as several pages of text at a time. Macy's books are full of this material, and there is more of it on his Web site—*www.worlditc.org.*

"Earth is gaining ever easier access to current descriptions of the afterworld," he writes, "complete with hard evidence to supplement the rich, religious descriptions of human heritage."

What we have learned so far is that the physical universe is but a small part of creation, that all worlds throughout this immense universe are composed of pure consciousness, and that the number one law of life everywhere is: Thoughts create reality. (Macy and Kubis, *Conversations Beyond the Light*)

This brings us to the biggest obstacle to undistorted two-way communication between dimensions. What we believe.

For instance, Timestream's facilities are located in the third plane of the astral world on a planet named Marduk. Believe that?

This mid-astral plane is called "the plane of illusion" because the forms and structures here are created by the collective thoughts, beliefs, and memories of its inhabitants. Believe that?

William James through Susy Smith said: "On the astral plane man makes his own environment."

A. E. Powell, in *The Astral Body*, writes: "Scenery on each sub-plane or division thereof represents the composite ideals and mental images of those inhabiting it."

Bob Monroe described the condition of like minds vibrating together in sympathetic frequency of shared belief. Birds of a feather flock together.

"Heaven is a dream world," Macy writes. "It's what you believe it is. However, it is as real to all the people who live there as our world is to us." Believe that?

"Thoughts create reality" applies on both sides of the veil. It is, in fact, the essence of spiritual growth. "Once a person is able to break through the idea boundaries"—to change their thinking—"a new type of existence is possible," Macy writes.

■   ■   ■

Let's return to the plight of the one who dies and does not know that he or she is dead. Let's say that's you. Imagine you are reading this page through the eyes of someone you've attached to who doesn't know you're there any more than you know that the body you are living through does not belong to you.

You do not know you are dead. You do not know the arms and legs you see in front of you belong to someone else, someone whose energy you are sapping by being in their field, someone who turns this page before you get to the bottom and is closing their eyes now, slumping in the chair, the book closing in their lap. They are asleep.

What do you do? You hang out, confused. Unaware of your condition, you are unable to separate from the reality you still seem to be part of but no longer have the ability to affect. You can't pick up the book and open to the page you were on. You can't read while the person you've attached to sleeps. But how can they sleep in the chattering commotion of voices you keep hearing? Where are these voices coming from? Who else can hear them? And when will they shut up?

The racket may be coming from other discarnate beings attached to your host who know no better than you do what is going on. Multiple attachment of the same host is common. "A living person can have dozens, even hundreds of attached spirits as they occupy no physical space," says Baldwin.

The disturbance, in fact, may be caused by entities you brought in yourself, entities that had attached to you without your knowledge long before you died. "Piggy-back obsession," Baldwin calls it, "a nesting of entities," evoking the image of Chinese boxes inside boxes of stacked souls.

Louise Ireland-Frey, M.D. describes it this way:

> Imagine that an old alcoholic who died and whose soul continued to haunt bars had been obsessed by the soul of another drinker who had died before, and who, in fact, had increased the old man's addiction and hastened his death. Then suppose that the two-in-one had managed to invade another customer in the bar . . . and obsessed him . . . . From then on, the guest would be entertaining not only his own desire for alcohol but also the thirst of the old alcoholic plus the thirst of the other in him, the one "nested" in the old man. (Ireland-Frey, *Freeing the Captives*)

The more confused and frustrated all this makes you, the more intensely you are likely to focus on *this* side of the windshield in the dense world of matter where you no longer belong. At any moment you could shift your attention, turn away from that which seems real on this side of the glass, refocus, and look through to the other side. So, why don't you?

"It's a matter of education," says Wally.

Maybe you were told there is no life after death, that when the lights go out, that's it they don't come on again. If that's what you believe, and then the lights do come on again, why would you think you were dead?

Maybe you believe that when you die you will come face to face with Jesus or St. Peter or God. You think you know what they will look like and you haven't seen them yet, so how could this be death?

Those who believe that death is an eternity of sleep may just not wake up at all.

Certainly, those who believe in eternal damnation in the cauldrons of flaming hell are going to pull back some from the possibility that death is here. They're going to do anything they can to stay close to the light of the living and continue to focus on the familiar, illusory world of form.

Because the church has dropped the ball, as Wally puts it. Because the culture is in denial, Elisabeth Kubler-Ross writes. Because nobody does what the Tibetan Buddhists did twelve hundred years ago, and because being dead is so much like being alive, multitudes who die try to continue to self-medicate. Alcoholics find drinkers, drug dependents find a fix, compulsive eaters latch onto compulsive eaters, and sex addicts crawl into bed behind those who share their cravings—each attempting to block their fear of death by continuing to blunt their perceptions.

All they need is a host, and in this culture at this time, hosts are everywhere. Addictive personalities take on hitchhikers with no more awareness than of having another drink or ordering a pizza, oblivious to the fact that many of their growing physical and mental difficulties may not be theirs at all, but may belong to the entities they have allowed on board.

How can this happen?

Wally's "Script for Hitchhikers," the template he uses when he speaks to spirits during entity-clearing sessions, goes like this:

You died without knowing what to expect, without being prepared. Instead of looking for the Light and your friends and relatives who had come to greet you, you kept your mind focused on this world. You didn't notice those who came to meet you. When you didn't, you failed to make the proper transition into the Light where you should be, in your own perfect spirit body, learning and growing. That was your first mistake.

Your second mistake was when you attached your-self to _____. That's when you started harming _____. At the very least you have been sapping _____'s energy.

Because you were not properly prepared to die, you took with you your anger, grudges, resentments, fears, feelings, bad habits, addictions, attachments, desires, lust, hang-ups, and maybe even some mental problems or physical ailments. All of your "stuff" now gets mixed up with _____'s thoughts, feelings, habits, and desires, causing problems of erratic behavior, fatigue, strange emotions, poor concentration, and general confusion.

Edith Fiore describes how the lower astral body of an entity blends with the etheric body of the living being to create a kind of blueprint for such characteristics belonging to the possessor that then transfer to the host.

This can be everything from migraines to PMS, edema, cramping, insomnia, obesity, hypertension, asthma, allergies, sciatica, hot flashes. Memory problems, too, can manifest, as well as lack of concentration, anxiety, fears, and phobias— phobias frequently related to the actual circumstances of the former death experience.

The chronic neck pain of one of Fiore's clients was elimi-
nated when the possessing spirit of a man who had hung himself was detached from the client and sent on his way.

In another case, a client's sudden fear of driving was traced
to a short stay in a hospital for elective surgery during which
she had been attached by the spirit of a suicidally depressed
young woman who had driven off the cliffs of the Pacific Coast
Highway in despair. She had screamed in fear all the way to the
water. Her body had been taken to the hospital morgue from
which her spirit separated and drifted to an upper floor where
it found Fiore's client still under anesthesia. Another Mary
Rose.

■   ■   ■

Spirit interference is almost universal in the human population. According to Baldwin, between 70 and 100 percent of the
population is influenced by one or more discarnate spirit entities at some time in their life.

Often, the dead are members of the family. In a clearing
conducted by Wally and Ruth, a San Pedro mother in her forties, stricken by multiple sclerosis, spent her final five years
"bedridden, going downhill," being tended to by loved ones,
notably her mother, her sister, and eldest son. In death, the
woman couldn't seem to let go of the son with whom she'd
been so close, so she hung around—perhaps with the best of
intentions to provide the kind of loving guidance she'd been
unable to give him while she was sick and dying.

As it happens, the son likely had a part in drawing her
spirit to him. In his grief, he may have welcomed her presence
without being aware of what was going on. This did him no
good. Her mothering presence kept him moody and confused,

suffering poor concentration in school, causing him to pull away from friends to spend isolated hours alone in his room, anxious and depressed.

Strong emotions create powerful vibratory fields that attract sympathetic frequencies. The sad draw sadness to them. Those who grieve too long for the dead can literally keep them from moving on by the strength of their emotions.

Intense emotions such as rage and anger and jealousy can actually motivate attachment. Many instances have been reported of spirits who stayed earthbound in order to exact revenge on those they believed were responsible for their own deaths or for the deaths of loved ones. Jealous spirit husbands and wives and lovers have remained for the express purpose of spoiling the sex lives of those they've left behind.

In the case of the San Pedro mother, her sticking around seems deliberate but not malevolent. She may believe that she has unfinished business with her son, that she needs to remain in order to help.

What if she can? If there's a chance she can help him and he needs the help and there is love between them, what is wrong with her attaching?

What is wrong with her attaching is that Mom is dead. There exists no conscious communication between her and her host. No conscious choice was made, no agreement struck. Their emotions have drawn them together. Their vibrations. And, though that may feel good to one or both of them for a while, without the conscious knowledge of what is taking place, there is no understanding, and both will suffer.

The son doesn't know that his foreign thoughts and feelings are coming from his mother. He is bewildered and confused by his own behavior. He may fear he's going crazy.

Because the mother's astral body has no physical energy of its own, her presence drains the son of his strength, and renders him susceptible to physical ailments in addition to the psychological uncertainties we've seen.

Also, if Mom ever wants to detach from him to move about on her own, she'll be unable to do so. She is imprisoned within him—again, due to the strength of the magnetic force between them, and because there is no conscious knowledge by either one of what is going on.

In fact, the very notion that she could help him or change things between them is in question. According to Fiore, earthbound entities remain exactly as they were at the moment of their deaths. "Throughout their stay in the physical world they do not change or profit from anything they experience."

Because their business is elsewhere.

As long as the mother is trapped on the lower astral plane, she'll be unable to progress on her own spiritual path.

There is no healthy upside to possession.

Every obsessing or possessing entity, without exception, needs to be expelled.

How?

How depends on the degree of possession and possession by whom. Or what.

10

Other and More

THE EARTHBOUND SOUL OF A DECEASED human being is the most common kind of possessing entity. But there are others.

The mind of another living human being can possess, as can a past life personality or shell. Elementals or so-called "nature spirits," devas, demons, aliens and boogies, thought forms and fragments—either the fragment of a thought from a living person or the fragmented personality of a discarnate being can all cause psychic interference, from harassment to obsession to full-scale possession.

As for *fragments*, Australian doctor Samuel Sagan insists that no possessing entity is ever a full human spirit. He says they are all "little chunks of astral matter" that break off when the astral body shatters at death.

In *Entity Possession* (1999), Sagan writes that the Chinese believed the human soul to be at least ten separate souls, not subpersonalities or different parts of one unified soul as talked about by Elmer Green, but literally separate "things" that come from different places, are held together only as long as the individual is alive, and separate at death, having different destinations.

Sagan describes the human being as comprised of four parts, which he groups into pairs. Our dense part is made up of the physical body and the etheric body (life force, prana, chi), which permeates the physical body like water does a sponge. The part of the etheric body that extends beyond the physical body we call the aura.

The less dense upper half of us is made up of the astral body, that layer in which thoughts and emotions are embedded, and the Self (or Higher Self) which Sagan calls Ego, around which he says the astral body "entangles itself like a spider's web."

Just as our higher consciousness separates from our physical and etheric bodies to travel during sleep, so does it abandon both entirely at the moment of death. The etheric body begins to dissolve. The physical body starts to rot. The nervous system shuts down and, with the end of physical-mental consciousness, "comes the end of the illusion of being one single person," Sagan writes. "The dead suddenly realize"—or in the case of earthbound spirits, *fail* to realize—"their real astral nature. They are a mob." (*Entity Possession*)

We explode. Our astral body shatters into countless fragments of emotions, impressions, personalities, and character traits. If a small fraction remains attached to the rarified light of the Higher Self, it may move on into spirit realms, while a bigger part crumbles into undifferentiated dust and disappears. Sundry other bits break off to drift away as fragments, some of which can attach to living human beings depending, again, on residual desires.

These aren't desires that can ever again be quenched, but phantom patterns of behavior that nevertheless continue to persist. The impossibility of ever satisfying these cravings without a physical body only adds to the frustration of the fragmented entity and the emotional turmoil of the host.

Sagan's point is that these attaching entities are *not* your Uncle Si or Aunt Edna in toto, but only fragments of their personalities and character traits.

Elementals, on the other hand, are beings that have never manifested in a physical body. Sagan calls these "nonphysical little beings that stand behind earth, water, air, or fire, or behind flowers, trees, or other plants." These remind me of the "nature spirits" described by Itzhak Bentov in *Stalking the Wild Pendulum* (1977).

"We know that matter is consciousness (or, if you prefer, *contains* consciousness)," Bentov writes. "This consciousness, if there is enough of it (a critical mass), will develop a dim awareness of self."

Over millions of years, and through interaction with other creatures, "this dim awareness may be strengthened into a sharper identity." Hence, rocks, trees, caves, mushrooms, plants like the peyote cactus, all of which at first were "nothing more than a space charge," can gain energy and develop a more definite form, even a humanoid form, according to Bentov.

> A thought is energy that causes the neurons in the brain to fire in a certain pattern. That naturally produces tiny currents along definite paths in the brain cortex that can be picked up with sensitive instruments through electrodes on the surface of the skull. In this universe no energy is lost . . . . [This] means that the energy of the thought was broadcast in the form of electromagnetic waves, and at the velocity of light into the environment and into the cosmos. (Bentov, *Stalking the Wild Pendulum*)

Peruvian miners used to sacrifice llamas to the spirit of a rich vein of copper in their copper mines. A cult came to life around a cactus plant, and the ego of the spirit of that plant grew strong on the thoughts of the people who focused on it.

Mescalito, the spirit of the peyote plant described by Carlos Castaneda in *The Teachings of Don Juan* (1968), has for hundreds of years been the focus of devoted thoughts and rituals of singing and chanting and a specific style of drumming, which often accompany the ingestion of the buds of the peyote cactus.

Mescalito played a large part in what became the consciousness movement of the 1960s and '70s. He and his psychotropic cousin, LSD, synthesized from the mold ergot, threw open the doors of perception for many of us. No less distinguished a man than the writer Aldous Huxley, author of *Brave New World* as well as *The Doors of Perception*, "one bright May morning" in 1954, "swallowed four-tenths of a gram of mescalin dissolved in half a glass of water and sat down to wait for the results."

"This isn't the real world," Wally tells me.

"This isn't the real world," I repeat.

"The real world is the spirit world. Materialism is a superstition and an illusion," he says.

"A superstition."

"An illusion."

"A consensus reality."

"You just think this is real." He raps his knuckles on the table. "The physicists say that it's almost all empty space. You can shoot neutrons through this table, they won't even slow down."

"And, if an atom was the size of an orange in your hand and you could blow up the orange to the size of the planet

Earth, the nucleus of the atom would be the size of a cherry pit or something."

"You know that."

"I took acid."

"You can see through it."

"I can see through that."

"I read a physics book and you do acid. Why do I have to do things the hard way?"

I wouldn't say dropping acid was the easy way, exactly. It did have the advantage of being experiential rather than intellectual. And of course, there were the colors. The "heightened sensorium." Synesthesia, which is what they call the ability to see sound and hear smells and smell colors, is a trip.

What LSD did was open me up to the reality that reality may be other and more than it's been advertised to be. I grew curious. What is consciousness? What is the mind? How many minds are there? Are all cells conscious? Are thoughts things? I know we all know more than we think we do. "All learning is remembering." I agree with Plato there. John C. Lilly said, "Whatever you believe to be true either is true or becomes true." That rings true. Is perception reality? Bruce Lipton says it is. He says that we perceive the environment as we believe it to be.

"You'll see it when you believe it" has been a New Age cliché since Ruth and Wally and I first sat around my parents' table. But Bruce Lipton is not New Age. He is a cellular biologist firmly grounded in science whose research demonstrates the molecular connection of how belief literally switches on the gene that creates the perception that determines our behavior.

Textbook wisdom has had it that our genes control everything from hair color to shoe size to susceptibility to cancer.

We inherit our genes, so if there's cancer in the family, we will get it, done deal. We are victims of heredity.

Not true, says Lipton.

The genes in our cells are equivalent to software programs on a disk in a computer. But, the behavior of our cells is not programmed by our genes. The behavior of our cells is continuously adjusting to signals coming in from the outside environment.

Here's how Lipton says it works.

The human body is a protein machine. Proteins differ from each other by the linear sequencing of their amino acids and the subsequent charge of those amino chains. Like charges repel. Opposite charges attract. This causes movement. When a protein moves it can do a job—like muscle contraction, or digestion.

Protein receptors on the surface of the cell membrane move to let in or keep out incoming signals from the surrounding environment depending on what the incoming signal (sunshine, hot air, chemicals, sound) is *perceived* to be. On the cellular level, perception controls behavior of the proteins in the following way.

If allowed in by the receptor, the environmental signal goes to the affector, which sends a secondary signal to activate the protein that expresses the desired behavior, the release of an enzyme, for instance.

The receptor and affector function together as a unit of perception, literally a switch. There's no DNA involved. There are no genes involved. According to Lipton, all we've got so far is stimulus/response.

But, if this secondary signal can't find the protein it needs to respond to our perception of the environment—say the protein is absent from the cell's protoplasm—then the signal goes to the nucleus of the cell where the DNA is. The DNA is the blueprint for making all proteins—the pattern drawer, he calls it.

Once inside the nucleus, the signal finds the right gene by binding to the right regulatory protein, causing the protein sleeve to slide back and expose the gene that the signal has been looking for. A messenger copy is made called RNA. It is this RNA copy of the gene that then expresses the behavior for the function in the cell.

Genes do not control biology.

We are not victims of our genes.

We select our genes to respond to the environment we think we're living in.

The good news/bad news, of course, is that perception and environment may be two different things.

More good/bad news: It has been discovered that there exist in every cell of the body what are now being called "genetic engineering genes," whose function is to rewrite other genes "when necessary."

Say your perception is that the world is toxic, dangerous, and a threat. "Genetic engineering genes" will rewrite the other genes to respond not to the actual environment (which may *not* be toxic, dangerous, and a threat), but to your perception of it.

More news. In this machine that is our body, all software programs are written either for the purpose of *growth* or for the purpose of *protection*. Either/or. That's it. A switch. We're either growing toward what we perceive to be good or protecting ourselves against what we perceive to be bad.

When a cell is in protection, it stops growing.

Here's why Lipton says that is. The strongest growth-promoting signal is love. The strongest protection-seeking signal is fear. The hypothalamus in the brain gauges all incoming signals. If a negative signal like fear comes in, the hypothalamus activates the pituitary gland, which immediately cranks the system into fight or flight mode. Hormones shoot out of the adrenals, causing blood vessels in the viscera to squeeze, which forces blood away from the heart, kidneys, liver, lungs, and stomach, out into the muscles of the arms and legs in preparation to fight or fly. And that is how the adrenal system protects us from lions.

Meanwhile, our immune system, designed to protect us from bacteria and viruses and "things that get under our skin," gets starved of blood and, consequently, shuts down.

Fear shuts off the immune system.

Since our "perceptions" may be accurate or inaccurate, they can more accurately be described as beliefs.

Our beliefs control our biology, not our genes.

Our beliefs control, select, and rewrite our genes.

By adjusting our beliefs, we can adjust our behavior, we can select different genes, we can rewrite our genes.

This is, in fact, what we are doing all the time. On the cellular level, in the protein realm, we are constantly selecting and rewriting genes according to what we believe is going on.

If we are victims, we are victims not of our heredity, but of what we believe to be true. Literally.

According to Lipton, we can turn this around. We can stop being victims. We can change our beliefs.

The standard New Age method of changing beliefs has for many years been positive affirmations. Wally used them early on. They work like this. Rather than tell ourselves that the world is going to hell in a handbasket, we tell ourselves that there is light and love and purpose and meaning in the world and that as bad as things may look, "I can hardly wait to see the good that will come from this."

Louise Hay and others have sold boxcars full of books and audiotapes that affirm that if we just tell ourselves that what we want to have happen has already happened, and repeat this over and over, it will happen.

The problem with affirmations is that sometimes they work and more often, they don't. Robert Williams, who teamed up with Bruce Lipton for the videotape *The Biology of Perception, the Psychology of Change*, says he knows why this is.

He says that we have been talking to the wrong mind.

Our beliefs are not held in the conscious mind. Our beliefs are held in the subconscious mind. In fact, *all* of our beliefs, attitudes, and values, everything we've been told or overheard since conception, since before we were conscious, lives and breathes in our unconscious mind. Along with everything the body knows about itself.

But wait. I've jumped ahead.

■   ■   ■

Most of the sources I've quoted so far have been books I read when they came out in the '70s, '80s, and '90s—books that Wally and Ruth and I referenced back and forth as we were living our separate, somehow oddly co-joined lives spiraling out across the universe in parallel directions. Adam Crabtree's *Multiple Man* was new to me. The fact that Colin Wilson wrote its introduction drew me into it with high expectations, which were met. I recommend it.

Crabtree states on page one that, "there is not just one, but many 'minds' operating simultaneously within each human being." He goes on to describe the differences between thought forms and fragments and second selves and spiritual possession and obsession and multiple personality. He begins with mesmerism and the discovery of the "divided consciousness."

In Vienna in the late 1700s, Franz Anton Mesmer came to believe that magnetism filled the universe as "a fluid." He believed that the human body is a magnet, and that a physician could "use his own body to affect the magnetic balance of that of his patient," thereby restoring the natural ebb and flow of vital "currents."

These are the same "currents" mapped five centuries ago by Chinese acupuncturists and since recognized in the West as the "subtle energies" behind Therapeutic Touch and Healing Touch and Reiki and Jin Shin and other energetic healing modalities in which the healer uses his or her body to affect the energetic balance of the healee.

In fact, the technique of "magnetic passes"—repeated downward movements of the hands over the length of the body used by contemporaries of Mesmer—is called "magnetic unruffling" in present-day Healing Touch. I've seen Ruth and Laurel do this many times to clear toxins from the aura of a client and to calm them.

In 1784, the technique was used to bring a man named Victor into the state of what was then called "magnetic sleep," or somnambulism, which we would now call hypnotic trance. What was discovered during the session with Victor came to be known as "divided" or "double consciousness."

There is a "second self" within each of us that can be contacted and talked with. It has its own memories, its own personal characteristics, its own sense of self "quite distinct from the ordinary waking state." It is that part of us with which hypnotherapists like Crabtree and Fiore establish their rapport.

"The second consciousness is the same as the hypnotic self," Crabtree writes.

■   ■   ■

What Ernest Hilgard calls The Hidden Observer and Ralph Allison calls The Inner Self Helper, doctors working with Billy Milligan called The Teacher. It is that part, person, personality, entity, consciousness, or "intelligence in the background" that is aware of all the personalities within a multiple personality and can be persuaded to cooperate in its treatment.

The Minds of Billy Milligan by Daniel Keyes flat-out blew me away when I read it. Billy Milligan was discovered to have split into twenty-four separate personalities, each without his knowing.

In fact, the original Billy hadn't been allowed to hold his own consciousness since trying to kill himself six years before when, in self-defense, the strongest of the alternate personalities intervened and pushed Billy to the rear.

In 1977, when he was indicted on three counts of kidnapping, three counts of aggravated assault, and four counts of rape in Columbus, Ohio, the "real Billy" wasn't even "home." It took months before doctors could draw him out, which they finally managed only with the help of The Teacher, who had refused to make himself known until after the verdict.

This was the first time in the history of American law that a defendant had been acquitted of major crimes because of insanity due to multiple personality.

Post-trial, with Billy safely ensconced in a mental hospital under the care of Dr. David Caul, The Teacher finally emerged. Only he knew the complete cast of characters, most of whom were unaware of what was going on because, according to

Crabtree, Billy suffered both "horizontal amnesia," which blocked awareness between the separate personalities in the present, and "vertical amnesia," which blocked out all memory of the past.

With the help of The Teacher, Dr. Caul's treatment led to the amalgamation of the entire group—from Arthur, the reasoned leader who spoke with a British accent and could communicate well with "the children," to Ragen, the Yugoslav "keeper of hate" who spoke, wrote, and read Serbo-Croatian and would kick serious butt whenever physical harm was threatened, to Adlana, the lonely lesbian hungry for female contact. Ironically, it was Adlana who was responsible for the rapes with which Billy had been charged.

Each alternate had come to life to deal with a particular "dangerous" emotion that Billy's core personality had refused to feel. Billy's healing required that his core personality learn to tolerate and fully inhabit the entire spectrum of possible emotions without ducking out and handing off to the alternates.

The Teacher was the last to fuse. Unlike the others, it was finally discovered that The Teacher did have emotions of his own, emotions that changed as circumstances changed. In fact, The Teacher could finally be understood to be Billy "all in one piece."

The Teacher was Billy unafraid.

■   ■   ■

Multiple personalities, second selves, thought forms, fragments, nature spirits, devas, elementals, the discarnate beings of people who die and do not know that they are dead . . .

With everything that spirit interference can be or be mistaken for, the Catholic Church still admits to only one: demonic possession.

From all accounts, there *are* demons out there—malevolent beings, interdimensional parasites, and boogies of all kinds. William Baldwin expanded his therapies to include the treatment of spirit attachment by alien extraterrestrials.

"There seems to be some kind of long-term genetic experimentation and manipulation in progress," Baldwin writes. Some of these ETs claim to be scientists gathering information on human life forms. Others declare they have come to take over the human race and that they're doing the bidding of dark energy forces who wait on nearby hovering spacecraft. Sometimes, even the leader of the ruling high council on the home world seems to speak through Baldwin's clients.

It's not lost on Baldwin how crazy this sounds.

> This channeled information could be totally fabricated by the client, consciously or unconsciously. It may be a product of the collective unconscious mind, triggered by a subliminal mass hysteria over an urban myth of alien domination. A more sinister possibility reflects the fears of the conspiracy theorists; the alien abductions may involve elements of our own government who have formed some kind of alliance with ETs, beings from other worlds or other dimensions. Equally repugnant is the possibility that the entire UFO/ET enigma might be nothing less, nor more, than field testing of mind control technology by earth's own intelligence agencies or military personnel. (Baldwin, *CE-VI: Close Encounters of the Possession Kind*)

Whatever this phenomenon may or may not be, it is what Baldwin began hearing come through his clients while in the altered conscious state. As always, he proceeded as if it were true.

The Holy See, on the other hand, seems to see only the Devil, Satan, Lucifer—that bodiless, genderless "Father of Lies and a Murderer from the Beginning," and sees exorcism as the treatment of choice: the violent expulsion of Satan from the body of "the accursed."

But, what are the classic signs of demonic possession? Fluency in unfamiliar languages? Violent reaction to seeing holy objects? Paranormal knowledge of events happening at a distance? Foul and blasphemous language? Violent convulsions?

These last two are symptoms shared by people who suffer epilepsy, Tourette's syndrome, and Parkinson's disease. Clairvoyance, or the ability to psychically see what lies beyond "normal sight," is now understood to be a latent human trait that can be developed with practice and is the basis of the art of remote viewing, which has been funded by the U.S. government and used by the CIA and military intelligence for decades. Fluency in unfamiliar tongues, as seen, can be a symptom of Multiple Personality Syndrome.

And as for me, if I were tied down, bound or straight-jacketed as described by Malachi Martin in *Hostage to the Devil*, then bellowed at in Latin by Roman Catholic exorcists armed with crosses and water vials and pictures of the Virgin, I, too, might have a violent reaction to holy objects.

But, let's say Catholic bishops never get it wrong. While we're at it, let's say no jury of peers ever sentenced an innocent man to death. Let's say that every chosen candidate for exorcism is truly possessed by the Devil and that every state-ordered execution (even in Texas) only puts to death an unrepentant psychopathic monster.

What happens to the "demon" that has been driven out of the body of the so-called "accursed"?

What happens to the soul of the human "monster"—and to the souls of any unknowing dead who may have attached to it—when the physical body is lethally injected, shot, hung, or electrocuted?

They are rendered *invisible*. And pissed.

> The victims of capital punishment, apart from the injury done to them by suddenly wrenching from the physical the astral body, throbbing with feelings of hatred, passion, revenge, and so forth, constitute a peculiarly dangerous element in the astral world. Unpleasant to society as a murderer in his physical body may be, he is clearly far more dangerous when suddenly expelled from his body; and, whilst society may protect itself from murderers in the physical body, it is at present defenseless against murderers suddenly projected on to the astral planes in the full flush of their passions. (Powell, *The Astral Body*)

Consider, instead, Bill Baldwin's approach. His conviction that every living being in the universe contains a spark of the Divine extended even to Lucifer and his legion of so-called demons.

First, Baldwin stripped these demons of religious and historical superstition by calling them dark force energies instead. He then addressed them directly, as Ruth did with schizophrenics, face to face, so they could see her lips moving and know that she was the one who was talking. This is no hallucination.

Baldwin asked them to look deep inside themselves to the eternal, indestructible spark of God-consciousness that he insists we all share.

They buck and moan. They are not human, they protest, they never have been, would not want to be. There is no light where they come from, and certainly none within them. They are here to do The Master's bidding, to wreak havoc and destruction.

"Yes, but," said Baldwin. "Think back. Recall."

And he would proceed to guide them through gentle conversation to their own first memory, their first experience of being, first flicker of consciousness, back to their initial encounter with the darkness they then chose to follow, back to the lie they swallowed-that there is no light within them; that they can be destroyed; that the light will cause them harm.

Baldwin was easy with the notion of where the help he said he got came from. "The Spirits of Light who assist may be archetypal or imaginary. They may also be real conscious beings, existing in a nonphysical reality." Whatever they are and however it works, Baldwin called them in to form a barrier of light around the session, and then requested that they bind the entity in "a capsule of Light"—and squeeze. As they squeezed, he would talk.

> **Baldwin:** *Turn and look deep inside yourself. Begin to focus deep inside. Tunnel to your center, to the very center of your being. What do you find?*
>
> **Client:** *Nothing, it's just dark.*
>
> **Baldwin:** *Keep looking. What did they tell you was inside you, at your center?*
>
> **Client:** *There is nothing there except darkness, hate.*
>
> **Baldwin:** *Keep looking. Through the darkness, through the layers of darkness. Keep looking, keep going, right into your center. What do you see there? Look carefully.*
>
> **Client:** *There is some light. Just a spark.*
>
> **Baldwin:** *They deceived you . . . . How does it feel to know they deceived you from the beginning?*
>
> **Client:** *I don't like it. I'm angry. They lied to me.*

Baldwin: *Would you continue to serve these masters who deceived you like this?*
Client: *No.*
(Baldwin, *Healing Lost Souls*)

Baldwin guided these life forms to the realization that they are, in fact, eternal spirits and cannot be destroyed, that they are beings of the very Light that they've been told to fear.

"And he got them to leave and to take their buddies with them," Wally said.

I think of Ruth.

> The schizophrenic is like a man permanently under the influence of mescalin, and therefore unable to shut off the experience of reality . . . which he cannot explain away because it is the most stubborn of primary facts, and which, because it never permits him to look at the world with merely human eyes, scares him into interpreting its unremitting strangeness, it's burning intensity of significance, as manifestations of human or even cosmic malevolence, calling for the most desperate of measures. (Huxley, *The Doors of Perception*)

The much-maligned, ultimately outlawed early LSD research attempted to model the schizophrenic condition. When the U.S. government shut down this legal research, it spawned an illegal black market drug trade that made outlaws of anyone interested in stepping through the Doors, myself included.

From the beginning, the clinical protocols of this scientific research stressed the importance of "set and setting," as well as the necessity for always having a guide. By slamming the door on these efforts, the government put the drugs in the streets and rendered all experimenters guideless.

Ruth had served as guide in her work with schizophrenics. She had always, as Baldwin did, addressed herself to the spark of Light within them, to "the healthy part," she calls it.

"When you talk with a person who is mentally ill, you're always listening for and going to the healthy part," Laurel told me. To what they mean, not what they say. Not to the content that can be psychotic rambling or the latent language used to cloak their fears. They will toss "word salad" at you, speak in the second or third person, and project their anger outward rather than say what they mean, which is: Do you care about me? Am I a person to you? "Because so often they are treated as non-persons, you know."

The emotional intensity around and behind the words a schizophrenic uses is what Ruth calls the feeling tone. It is this feeling tone she always listened for and chose to speak to in her psychiatric work. It is the same indestructible spark of God-consciousness Baldwin spoke to, that selfsame spark of the divine that flickers in all life.

So, for all the schizophrenics and second selves and fragments and multiples and thought forms, elementals, nature spirits, dark force energies, and for all the people who die and do not know that they are dead:

> Let there be a voice to assure them that in spite of all the terror, all the bewilderment and confusion, the ultimate reality remains unshakably itself and is of the same substance as the inner light of even the most cruelly tormented mind. (Huxley, *The Doors of Perception*)

11

It Started in Naples When Laurel's Mother Died

LENA DIED THE DAY BEFORE WALLY and Ardis got there. The four of them were sitting around Ruth and Laurel's table. "We just asked if her mother had gone to the Light and the pendulum said no," Ardis told me. "Wally and I had just read the Edith Fiore book with the procedure for sending souls to the Light, so we decided to try it, and discovered that Laurel's mother had gone into her roommate's body at the nursing home." Lena had attached herself to Opal.

"It began with Lena," Wally said. "I was aware of the pendulum as a source of Universal Knowledge if you know how to use it and what questions to ask, so why not ask it that?"

"We were sitting around in a circle," Ruth told me, "and we were talking about things and I picked it up and it started responding to the questions that Wally would have asked Lorraine if she had been there. Questions like "Are there hitchhikers? Does so-and-so have a hitchhiker? Who is it?" Questions that a psychic would be able to answer as far as who that entity was. We just tried it out and found that the pendulum could be the feedback that Wally had previously gotten from Lorraine. We were tapping into the same thing."

The pendulum takes the place of the psychic.

"So, we cleared Lena's roommate, and then started asking about various other family members," Ardis said.

"Here's where we started." Wally pulled out a folder of notes: "February 15, 1995. Lena died, went to Opal, we sent Lena to the Light and then began healing energy transmission to Mona, Bob, Aunt Edna, Shirley. Pete-somebody was attached to Shirley. Six foot, seventy years old, followed Shirley and her son home fourteen years ago. Her therapist had some, too. Smoker, eater. Corrie had Donald's grandmother. Mona had a 'motherly type for forty years.' Healing for Mona, filled with light. Norene, five entities—Uncle Harry, Roscoe, Professor Schwenk, and two other males. Leland, twelve, ten from Stromsburg and two from Bend. Stromsburg was where he had his tonsils out. That's when they put him under. Probably picked up from the hospital there. Faith, five, including Grandma Dot and four of her patients. See, nurses pick them up."

Wally cracked a smile. "I thought I'd created this business of clearing hitchhikers with the pendulum. But a year later I found a book that I had read three years before and it was all laid out in there. I'd even underlined it."

The book was *Exorcism: How to Clear at a Distance a Spirit-Possessed Person* by Eugene Maurey.

■   ■   ■

Let's go back. Last time we saw Ruth she had just signed up for Level 1 of Healing Touch in Raleigh. She had bought her first pendulum, and by the time she and Wally got back to Portland, she had decided to say no to radiation and chemo. The oncologist told her she'd be dead in two years. No one knows if that oncologist is still alive or not. No one remembers his name. But eight years later, Ruth was using her pendulum as an information dowser to detach earthbound spirits at a distance.

Ruth had attended Level 1, then Levels 2 and 3, was certified to practice and later to teach. She started working closely with the founder, Janet Mentgen. Janet was a psychic. Some of the techniques she had folded into Healing Touch had come to her in dreams. She had to draw in her aura at the airport, they said, or she would set off alarms. Cats liked her, I remember. I never got to know her well. There was a gnomelike quality to Janet, like a forest critter, a hoarder of nuts. She and Ruth got along very well at the start.

Ruth really took to Healing Touch. Having taught all her life and with a solid medical background, she soon proved to be a natural healer as well. Ruth "has hands," is the expression, and is gifted with the ability to stay out of the way, to remove herself from expectation of outcome, and to allow the healing energy to go where it is needed, which is key.

The prana, chi, soul, life force energy that moves through both healer and healee "belongs" to neither of them. It is not theirs either to rudder or possess. To try to muscle an outcome is a way to fail at energy work and a certain route to burnout.

"When ego gets in the way and it becomes more important to be the healer that makes this happen than to let it happen, you're no longer really doing the work," Ruth said. "To be able to go into an 'allow mode' requires that you set aside your ego and that you set aside outcomes and that you operate from the standpoint of what's in the best interest of the individual, the highest good of the individual."

The same is true for using the pendulum to clear earthbound spirits, true for using the pendulum at all. "Thy Will Be Done" has been found to be a more effective prayer than prayers to "cure" someone.

In fact, making the distinction between curing and healing is essential in energy work. "Curing" is the cessation of physical symptoms. "Healing" is an ongoing process that involves the growth of the whole human being toward finding a balance between their physical, mental, emotional, and spiritual bodies. That goes for the healer, too.

Janet was a psychic and not particularly interested in the conceptual planking that supported her healing art. As a teacher, Ruth believed in the need to expose those moving through the program to enough historical background and source information to provide them with a context for their healing practice as well as their own personal process. To do anything less was to set yourself up as a guru, and "guru-ism does not enhance inner development," said Ruth. "The minute you set up a guru situation, you stop growth."

Growth continued for those who split off from Healing Touch through the formation of the Holistic Alliance of Professional Practitioners, Entrepreneurs, and Networkers, Inc. (HAPPEN) and the development of a curriculum called Transformational Pathways. Inspired by the principle, "all healing is self-healing," this curriculum provided the conceptual framework missing with Healing Touch. It surveyed the current health system, compared Eastern and Western approaches, delved into theoretical physics, considered the mind and consciousness, and shifted focus from technique alone to a broader context for understanding health and healing and spiritual growth.

We believe that all healing is self-healing and that self-healing is at the heart of healership. Within the rich evolution of Allopathic and Eastern health care approaches, the curriculum is on the cutting edge in presenting discoveries and providing awareness of self-healing within the context of ancient wisdom. The

concepts of the subtle energy system, holism, transpersonal perspective, holistic communication and healership are woven throughout. (Johnston, "Transformational Pathways" brochure)

The emphasis placed on self-care as part of self-healing included
"learning to listen to one's own body as a source of information."
Ruth had been doing this since deciding "to do only those things
purported to enhance immune function" when she said no to
radiation and chemo—by consulting her pendulum.

"It is the fastest turnoff for many people of your reliability,
your use of a pendulum," Laurel said. "It's very New Age."

Still, Ruth has been doing it since 1987. "It is the major way
I am in touch with my body. And the more I use it the less I
need it, in one sense."

In restaurants, Ruth pendles menus. At the grocery store,
she pendles eggs and melons. At home, she asks how many
cherries can she eat. Can she have ice cream? How much time
on the stationary bike?

"Would it be healthy for me to walk today? I had been asking
in terms of distance—how many times around the lake—and
that was fuzzy. When I started asking in relation to time, I started
getting clearer answers. Would it be healthy for me to walk for
ten minutes? Twelve minutes? And so forth, until I hit the 'no,'
and then I back off and reconfirm the one before," she said.

Determining diet and exercise with a pendulum is one thing,
more like choosing a plumber from the yellow pages, which she
also does. Using the pendulum to diagnose physical ailments or
choose healthcare providers or decide which supplements to take
in what combinations for how long seems like belief of another
magnitude, but this is what Ruth does. Now with help.

"I thought I was looking for an acupuncturist," Ruth said,
when a member of HAPPEN recommended Dr. Wright.

Dr. Wright is "an M.D. whose specialty is environmental toxins who also has training in acupuncture, homeopathy, and she's an herbalist and took training for microcurrent," which at the time Ruth knew nothing about.

From a meridian assessment, Dr. Wright determined that Ruth was suffering from mercury toxicity caused by the amalgams in her teeth. She'd been having trouble with her hip, with lymphoma, and had recently begun to have a droopy eyelid. Wright diagnosed the droopy eyelid as myasthenia gravis and sent her to a Dr. Hansen in Fullerton, California, who began removing the mercury from her mouth.

"I firmly believe that it's the mercury toxicity that has created all these things," Ruth told me. "And when I learned about the meridians and the relationship between the teeth and the mammary glands, I don't think there's any question that the amalgams in the teeth that related to the left mammary gland had something to do with that cancer."

Now, a second cancer, eleven years after her first oncologist had pronounced her dead, was found in her right breast.

"In June of 2000, the meridian assessment made it clear that the upper-right quadrant of my mouth was the highest priority for attention." Dr. Hansen chose to work on the lower-left instead. "Well, in May of 2001, I developed the cancer in the right breast. Call that coincidence if you'd like, but that seems pretty direct to me, and what I kept getting from the pendulum was don't let them biopsy till after the dental work has been done because a biopsy will stir up what is going on."

So, Ruth held off from May until September for the surgery. Because of what she "kept getting from the pendulum," and because of what had happened that first time she'd gone in to see Dr. Wright.

"The first time I saw her she did a complete physical workup, a combination of traditional Western intake and an energetic intake using kinesiology for figuring out what supplements I needed and so forth."

Kinesiology is muscle testing, a system of feedback from the body itself, a method used to connect with what the body knows about itself. "Cell knowledge," said Laurel. "Every cell in your body knows what's going on in every other cell of your body."

"It is consciousness in the broadest sense," said Ruth. "If you don't get in its way, and maybe if you believe it, kinesiology and dowsing and the pendulum, I think, are all related. It all has as its basis the fact that we are one and that we can be in touch"— with what we know, with what is known. "I believe that it taps into universal knowledge. Wally believes that it taps into universal knowledge." Evidently, so did her new doctor.

Dr. Wright had Ruth hold small, unmarked vials containing homeopathic solutions of different calcium preparations. (A homeopathic substance is the dilution by water of that substance to the point where not one single molecule of the substance itself remains. It is its energy.) One by one, the doctor asked herself silent questions about the contents of each vial as she had Ruth resist the gentle downward pressure she placed on Ruth's outstretched arm. When Ruth's deltoid muscle either "let go" or "locked in," she had her answer—a strong response meant "yes," a weak response meant "no."

"She put something in my hand but I didn't see what it was," Ruth said, "and I didn't know what questions she was asking herself about it. Then, when she left the room, I checked the bottles with my pendulum. Out of five little vials, four of them were rejected and one was accepted."

Independent of each other, they got the same results. "Right on the nose. What was good for me to take, what wasn't, dosage, the whole shebang. Independently. I was wavering a little bit in relation to how much I believed in my pendulum until Dr. Wright affirmed it so strongly and told me that she hoped I would be able to find other healthcare practitioners who would work with me that way."

Ruth did. Dr. Carolyn McMakin soon became as important to Ruth as Eileen Wright. Dr. Carol, Ruth calls her, specializes in Frequency Specific Microcurrent. It is an electrical treatment that delivers current measured in millionths of an amp, which is the same subsensory rate at which our bodies produce energy of their own in each cell.

According to the literature, Frequency Specific Microcurrent has the ability to relieve pain and increase production of the body's own chemical energy, ATP, as much as five hundred percent. It also "improves protein synthesis and amino acid transport, increases the rate of wound healing, stimulates the regeneration of injured tissues, stimulates lymphatic flow, relieves myofascial trigger points, and changes scar tissue."

It does this through *biologic resonance*. It matches the specific vibratory rate of the tissue, organ, organ system, or physical condition to a frequency setting on the microcurrent machine. Each protocol is triggered by the setting of a different number.

Dr. Carol wanted to start with frequency settings that would increase Ruth's circulation in order to begin to dump the mercury toxins from her muscles and tissues. She'd need to decide how long to spend at each setting.

To help determine this, Ruth pulled out her pendulum. At the same moment, Dr. Carol pulled out her own. From then on, they have functioned as like-minded compatriots, and along with Eileen Wright in Asheville, North Carolina, have consulted, considered, researched, searched the Web, confirmed, diagnosed, made adjustments, and kept all questions open.

"It is important to state that, short of dissection or tissue biopsy," writes Dr. Carol, "we don't know whether the frequencies we use are actually doing what we think they are doing. What we do know is that when we use them within a certain conceptual framework patients who had been symptomatic, sometimes for years, failing with both conventional and unconventional treatments, recover."

Here are three professional women who are comfortable with ambiguity and willing to take the responsibility to act as if something glimpsed but not yet proven may, in fact, be true. They have become Ruth's healthcare team.

"A lot of people don't really want to participate in their own healthcare," said Ruth. "You live a longer life if you do, for a lot of reasons, but you have to want to take that responsibility."

True to character, Ruth decided to find out all she could about Frequency Specific Microcurrent by signing up for Dr. Carol's core seminar. In fact, Ruth and Wally entered the field as colleagues. Wally bought the machine and Ruth paid for her training, after which she began to work on herself and Laurel and Ardis and Wally and other members of the family, including me.

I was stretched out on the massage table late one afternoon in Wally and Ardis's front room when Ruth got back from an appointment with Dr. Carol.

"You know what?" Ruth said, putting down her bag. "There's microcurrent frequencies for the removal of entities. The frequencies are listed under 'tendency to have chronic pain.'"

How did that come up?

"I was telling Carol, 'Where are you in relation to hitch-hikers?' And she laughed and she said, 'Well, since you're going to ask me that, I'll tell you about the six-tens. We can remove parasites with microcurrent.'"

"Parasites in the sense of—"

"I think what she's run into are the little malevolent ones which a clairvoyant she worked with saw as 'spiders and snakes.'"

"Hitchhikers."

"Hitchhikers."

Ruth disappeared into the bathroom and came out with a shallow bowl of water.

"I learned some more for you, too," she said. "I've got some things to add to your protocol."

Ruth dipped two black rubber gloves into the bowl, put one against the skin of my lower back and the other on my stomach, wires leading from the gloves to the microcurrent machine, then started flicking settings.

"The fact that you can clear them with the microcurrent is intriguing to me."

She pulled her pendulum out.

"She's run the frequencies on me a couple of times, but she doesn't talk about it unless somebody brings it up. She said, 'We try to keep the clinic clear, but you can't always keep it clear.' She said a lot of this information will come out in the advanced course, so I'm real anxious to take the advanced course in November," and she lifted her voice toward Wally in the living room. "I'll be down here for that," she said.

The pendulum swung wide in a clockwise direction. Ruth laughed. "It seems to think that's a good idea." She shakes her head.

"Carol's used to my pendulum joining in the conversation. Like when she was getting answers that she didn't expect, she looked at the pendulum and said, 'Are you for real?' And the thing just went—"

The pendulum whirled wide. We both laughed.

12

Six Hundred Hitchhikers

IN THE VAULTED CENTRAL ROOM OF A MANUFACTURED home on a side street in northeast Portland, Oregon, Wally and Ardis and Laurel and Ruth and I sit around the dining room table. Were it daytime, sunlight would be flooding in around us. Lush leafy green plants would be respiring audibly. It is night.

"We are speaking to you, Charley Hoop. You are in Lyle Hoop's body, a body which does not belong to you, Charley. Your own body is dead. This may come as a surprise to you, but we have learned that being dead is so much like being alive that many people have died without realizing their condition."

Charley and Lyle lived together in the same house for many years, and when Charley died, he simply continued on without realizing that he was dead or that he had attached himself to Lyle, his son. The men were "unchurched" (Ardis's word), and had no idea of what to expect or even much curiosity about death. Both men worked with their hands and rarely read a book, certainly none of those referenced in the one you are reading.

Wally knew Lyle and Charley and had responded to the son's complaints of fatigue and depression and confusion that had gripped him since his father's death several months before. Wally called Ruth, Ruth asked the pendulum, and the pendulum said yes, Lyle'd been attached.

A week or so later, when Ruth and Laurel were down from Seattle where they now lived, the five of us sat down and did a clearing. It went well. Wally described the situation to Charley and Charley didn't resist. "It is a mistake for you to attach yourself to Lyle because it fatigues him. It discourages him. It mixes your feelings and your hang-ups with his. You do not belong there." Wally turned to Ruth. "Does Charley understand that he is in a place where he does not belong?" The pendulum circled clockwise and Wally went on.

He told Charley to look around, find a spot of light and call out to someone who he knew who was dead and who cared about him. "Call to them and then just float to the light," he told him. "You don't even have to walk over there. There will be people there to greet you and to show you how things work." Wally told him that he could come back and check in with Lyle once in awhile, but "you are not to come back and stay in his energy field and sap his energy and confuse him."

Charley moved on. The pendulum confirmed it. But, before Lyle's clearing, the pendulum had told us that in addition to Charley, Lyle's aura was harboring three other entities—fragments of some kind, thought forms or dark energies. These had either come in nested with Charley or were part of Lyle's psychic baggage from before his father died. In any event, they were still there and needed to go. Never having lived in a human body, they would not be given to reason. Wally could talk himself blue. There was only one thing to do. Call Lord Michael and the Mercy Band of Rescue Angels.

Believe that?

■   ■   ■

Sashay was her stage name and her stage was very small. In fact, it sometimes was a table top; often, a lap. She was an exotic dancer at a gentleman's club, and she'd been attached by earthbound spirits.

Sharon was her real name. Sharon drank, did drugs, was hip-deep in an abusive relationship, had both a restraining order against her boyfriend and a new set of keys for him. Sharon was conflicted. Her mother knew Wally. Wally said he would help.

So, Wally, Ardis, Ruth, Laurel, Sharon's mother (a bit of a psychic), and I sat around the dining room table. Together, we created the bubble of light, we said the prayer. "And now, using the pendulum," Wally started, "let's ask how many entities are hitchhiking on Sharon."

"Seven," said Ruth.

"Seven. And now let's ask the pendulum: Are all of these earthbound entities spirits who have at one time lived in a human body?"

Ruth read the clockwise movement. "Yes," she said.

"Yes. And now with the pendulum let us ask Universal Intelligence for permission to work on the Higher Self of Sharon."

Ruth nodded.

"Permission granted. Now, we call into this bubble of light the Higher Self of Sharon and any and all entities that may be attached to the body or the energy system of Sharon. Are they present?"

"Yes."

"To Sharon's Higher Self: Do we have permission to instruct these attached entities on how and why they should make a proper transition to the spirit world?"

Asking permission of the person's Higher Self is important because?

"It could be part of that person's journey that that hitch-hiker is there, at least at that present time," Ruth said. "This is not something we are doing *to* the person. It's a facilitation of what that person's Higher Self truly wants, a recognition of that person's own journey and the sacred nature of the Higher Self."

"And we do that work in the name of God," said Laurel.

"It's all spiritual work," Ruth agreed, "but the difference between this and most religious work is that we don't deem to know what's best for everybody. It's not *our* values. It's the individual's values that are recognized and honored."

"Even if the individual is totally unaware of what we're doing?" I asked.

"That's right," Ruth said, "because we contact the Higher Self."

"We have permission from Sharon's Higher Self," said Wally. "And now we speak to each and every hitchhiking entity: You are in Sharon's body, a body which does not belong to you. It belongs to Sharon. Understand that your own body is dead."

Wally started to tailor his script on the fly: "At one time each of you hitchhikers had your own physical body. Then something happened—an illness, an operation, an accident, maybe a drug overdose, maybe murder or suicide."

Hell, maybe a bar fight or a knifing, I thought, as Wally pitched his script to the obvious suspects—the alcoholic, angry, lonely, confused, depressed, substance-abusing low-vibration spirit clientele at the topless bar where Sharon worked.

"You may have seen your ill or mangled body from a place above it. You may remember hearing someone say, 'We've lost him' or 'She's gone.' You may have tried to yell at them, 'No, I'm not gone, I'm right here, I'm okay.' But nobody could hear you. You may have tried to touch people, only to have your hand go through them. These are all certain signs that you are dead."

Existing only in their spirit bodies now, Wally told them, they had died unprepared, without knowing what to expect. They hadn't known enough to look to the Light or to the loved ones gathered there to meet them and, instead, they latched onto Sharon, and took with them their anger, fears, resentments, addictions, desires, "maybe even mental problems or physical ailments"—which now are all mixed up with Sharon's stuff.

Wally paused for emphasis.

"Maybe you think you've done some terrible things. You may be afraid to go to the other side, afraid that you'll be judged and condemned to burn in Hell forever. But thousands of people have been clinically dead and come back. Some have gotten into scary places, but mostly they tell us that you can expect a life review where everything you've done will flash before your eyes along with all the feelings, good and bad, that you have triggered in others. If you've been real nasty, this could be a kind of hell to feel the pain you've caused, but the purpose of the life review is not to punish you, but to help you understand. The only judgment on the other side is self-judgment. There is no punishment. The Light is a world of unconditional love and acceptance, whether you think you deserve it or not.

"So, now, through the pendulum, I ask all entities: Are you ready to go to your rightful place in the spirit world where you can have your own perfect spirit body and be with the friends you had before, where you can learn and grow?"

Wally turned to Ruth. The pendulum was spinning counterclockwise. They were saying no. And these weren't thought forms or fragments or dark energy tangles. These were human spirits either too strung-out to answer or adamant about staying put. No.

Wally tacked right and continued to persuade. No deal. He tacked left, describing still more of what he believes to be true, and got nothing.

Finally, the only thing to do, as with Lyle Hoop, was to call on Lord Michael and the Mercy Band of Rescue Angels, which, I repeat, is not a British punk rock group that played at CBGB's in the early 1980s.

■   ■   ■

I have put off describing Lord Michael because, frankly, I don't know what to make of angels. They live outside what Wally would call my giggle box. My image of angels is the female figure with great feathered wings on the back of the fans in the pews at the Warren Methodist Church of my youth. She floats above a small bridge where two curly-headed, very Anglo children skip, holding hands.

Or Bruno Ganz in Wim Wender's movie *Wings of Desire*. He and Otto Sander move about in a black-and-white Berlin, their hair pulled back into ponytails, wearing long black coats. They're at your shoulder in the library, they hear everybody's thoughts, they move through walls. Bruno Ganz falls into such love with a human trapeze artist that he surrenders immortality to physically embrace her, to make love, to taste coffee.

There's also Clarence in *It's a Wonderful Life* and that bell ringing every time an angel gets its wings. And John Travolta in *Michael*. And *Angels in America*. Maybe I've seen them depicted too many times too many ways without ever having met one. Or, without being conscious of ever having met one. Maybe the room is full of them and I don't know it.

Ethereal beings. Never having lived as humans. Two came to Drunvalo Melchizedeck when his name was still Bernard Perona. In fact, they brokered his transition to holy man, unless I got that wrong. Oh, and Jean Luc Godard. In his movie *Hail Mary* he casts Archangel Gabriel as a jet-lagged thug with a three-day beard in a long dark overcoat who pummels our friend Joseph in a hotel room where Mary has finally agreed to show Joseph her breasts. Joseph pleads, "Why can't I see them?" Gabriel answers, "Because it's the Law." Pow!

> Supernatural beings who have great intelligence and power. Guiding influences and spirits who watch over each soul in embodiment. Generally regarded as good, innocent, powerful, and beautiful, and may intervene to protect us from harm. There is a hierarchy within the angelic realms that constitutes many levels of power: Angels, Archangels, Principalities, Powers, Virtues, Dominions, Thrones, Cherubim, and Seraphim.
> (Milanovich and McCune, *The Light Shall Set You Free*)

At East/West Books in New York City, at Isis in Denver, at The Way Home in Lincoln, Nebraska, there are laminated portraits for sale of Ascended Masters—Quan Yin, Serapis, Kuthumi, Mother Mary, St. Germaine, Gabriel, Ariel. In the portrait of Lord Michael, he wields a wide shiny sword.

Angels.

Suddenly, I think of Mark Macy and the Polaroid pictures of spirits he takes in the subtle energy field produced by his Luminator machine. According to Macy, the Luminator "opens things up" between dimensional realms, thus encouraging an intermingling of beings from less dense worlds into our own—spirits, guides, earthbound entities, and angels.

The only modification to the camera he uses is a black strip of tape he's placed over the flash bar in which he's cut a hole "the size of a sesame seed." This reduces the amount of light bounced off his subjects. Otherwise, his camera is off the shelf. Results vary.

On the afternoon I spent with him at the Association for Research and Enlightenment (ARE) in New York in May of 2004, Macy snapped several pictures of each person there, standing in front of a large potted plant. Some pictures came up clear, in focus, conventional. Others came up blurry, as if he'd jiggled the camera. Still others came up in focus, but streaked with anomalous smears of light. Several looked like double exposures, which is technically impossible with a Polaroid camera because its shutter opens only once for each exposure.

But, the truly amazing shots, and I saw several, showed faces or parts of faces superimposed over the faces of the workshop member posing for the snapshot. Some of these faces were more distinct than others, most of them looking out toward the camera, others in profile. The faces resemble gelatinous see-through masks with human features, usually covering half the face, sometimes the whole face, sometimes recognized as family or loved ones, sometimes not.

They could be spirits who just happen to be passing through the room, Macy said. Or spirit guides or entities you don't know you have and so don't recognize, but that travel with you. Many times, he said, they may be something that came in with him— one of his guides or an angel, an ethereal being.

A woman named Debbie in the group I was in had three pictures taken. The first one came up normal, slightly soft. In the second, the dimensions of her face seemed rounder, swollen, as if filling up with fluid. When the third image came up, Debbie gasped. Clearly superimposed over her chin and neck was the face of a man in his late forties, early fifties, facing forward and smiling. Tears streamed. It was Debbie's husband, nine weeks dead. Debbie'd come from Philadelphia with her girlfriend on a mission to see Mark, having read all of his books and thoroughly plumbed his Web site. She wanted proof that John was with her.

Between the afternoon and evening sessions, Debbie'd gone out and had the picture blown up. Enlarged and compared to a happy snapshot she'd brought of the two of them hugging under trees in a suburban driveway, the resemblance was unmistakable. He was there. They were together.

"He was there."

Where is that, exactly? How do these worlds superimpose, again? How does this intermingling take "place"?

Being "outside" time, the other side is also "outside" space. What separates these worlds one from another is the difference in the frequency at which their matter vibrates. This is what Itzhak Bentov says, and Drunvalo Melchizedek, and A. E. Powell, and Instrumental Transcommunication pioneer George W. Meek, who was a friend and working colleague of Macy's before he died. Meek was, in fact, the one who brought Macy into the work, and who, shortly after his death in 1999, started working with Macy again, this time from the other side.

While visiting Macy and his wife at their home near Boulder, a psychic friend from New York clairvoyantly saw George Meek "working fastidiously from the other side of the veil with Radio #3." Meek had at his side ITC supporter and past president of the Institute of Noetic Sciences (IONS), Willis Harman, who died in 1997. The psychic saw these two men literally *in Macy's lab*, doing work on their equipment *superimposed over the equipment in Macy's space.*

This reinforced Macy's own understanding that "the spirit worlds are right here in the room with us at all times. Apparently our spirit friends assemble their equipment right over our telephone. They make our phone ring, we pick it up, and they talk to us." The circuits are activated not by a signal coming through the public telephone network (which shows no record of these calls), but "by signals created by invisible hands operating invisible devices," says Macy.

George Meek had described how this works to Macy back in 1991:

> You know this room is filled with radio signals, right? And you know that each signal remains distinct by its frequency. That's why a radio can tune separately to each signal. Well, all the spiritual universes—and there are hundreds of them—they're all sharing this space with our physical universe, like radio signals sharing the room. (Macy, *Miracles in the Storm*)

Macy goes on to write that

> The room is also filled with many types of invisible beings, from ghosts to angels, that move in and out of our lives all day everyday. Those which have the most profound effect on us are those who resonate with our thoughts, feelings, and attitudes. People on Earth draw into their lives spirit beings of like attitude. Love and empathy expressed by people on Earth are fueled by the support of loving and empathetic spirit beings. Conversely, resentment and fear felt by individuals on Earth are fueled by the eager support of negative spirits. (Macy, *Miracles in the Storm*)

Macy is convinced that ITC's ongoing two-way communication with spirit colleagues could not happen without the choreography of an ethereal cluster of angelic beings he calls The Seven. Spirit colleagues committed to communicating with us must stay in the lowest, densest levels of the astral planes closest to the Earth in order to message back and forth. This has never been simple and is growing more difficult. Even with The Seven serving as liaison between us, contacts all but dried up in the years between 1997 and 1999.

Konstantin Raudive, now working from the other side, sent a message in May of 1994: "ITC can only work when the minds of those involved are resonant and ethically pure." Again, in August, he warned that, "it can only work when the vibrations of those present are in complete harmony and when their aims and intentions are pure."

"The problem is vibrations," Wally said. "My theory, and I wrote to Mark Macy about this, was I think there is a certain frequency for love. This is a carrier wave. Other information can be superimposed on it, either amplitude or frequency, but if you don't have love on both ends, the same frequency on both ends, if there's jealousy on one end, if there's jealousy or ego involvement on the other end, it isn't going to work. You have to have love on both ends or the carrier wave breaks down and you don't get the transmission.

"What he said was, 'I like the way you think, Wally.'"

Spirit communication comes through technological devices on Earth, but has more to do with subtle energy forces such as chi, thought, intention, and love, which "lie outside the electromagnetic spectrum and beyond the view of science," than it has to do with hardware, says Macy. It has everything to do with harmony and resonance in the *contact field*.

"It's all about the field," says Macy.

Angels.

Do they bounce light? Can you take a picture of one? Can you prove they exist?

"To focus on proof is to focus on doubt," the spirits tell Macy, and that doesn't interest them. In fact it blocks their efforts. Doubt is a wall. Fear blocks miracles. What you believe is what you get. The observer is part of the experiment. Uri Geller can't bend spoons with his mind if he's surrounded by doubters. Does that mean Uri Geller is a fraud? Or that the phenomenon he's part of involves subtler forces than can be seen? measured? repeated? proven?

"People on Earth draw into their lives beings of like attitude."

Is Debbie's photograph "proof" that John was there? Thoughts are things. Could Debbie's husband have been the materialization of Debbie's intense desire and willful intention to have him with her? Was John a thought form? Do thought forms bounce light? Can they be photographed? If that's what happened at ARE, if that is how that photograph I saw came into being, I say that's only slightly less miraculous and certainly no less interesting than if he actually showed up in the room. Who knows?

"The miracle is to walk upon the earth," after all. I forget who said that, but Einstein's quoted somewhere saying "There are only two ways to live your life; One is as though nothing is a miracle. The other is as if everything is. I believe in the latter," and that is what I choose.

I choose to focus on ITC's long string of miracles, from the faint, squeaky voices of early tape recordings, to color pictures and pages of text that appear in the files of computers that were left turned off, to two-way telephone conversations lasting many minutes full of technical advice from spirit colleagues about how to modify equipment on this side, back to the early burst of images flashed on a TV screen that showed "mountains, a forest, a building, . . . a couple walking hip-deep out into a lake or ocean holding hands, then releasing hands, then joining hands again" and the high-pitched voice that broke through static "to announce the end of this successful experiment—the transmission of pictures 'live' from the astral world Marduk."

Believe that? I do.

An early ITC picture shows Hollywood film director George Cukor sharing lab space with a young Tom Edison. Nikola Tesla is working there. And Madame Curie. Robert Monroe dropped by. And Jules Verne, the long-dead author of *Around the World in Eighty Days*, sent Luxembourg a three-page fax!

That cracks me up. I'm not sure why. I don't apologize for laughing. I join Raymond Moody laughing. "That's why they call it paranormal!" says Moody in his book, *The Last Laugh*, which you should read.

Moody complains that the logjam blocking meaningful investigation into life after death and things paranormal is caused by the vested interests of professional parapsychologists, and the vested interests of professional skeptics, and the vested interests of fundamentalist Christians who claim it's all the work of the Devil.

"I believe we are entranced by the paranormal because we are entertained by it," Moody writes. That doesn't mean it isn't true. Just that it can't be proven. That's the point. That's the funny part. It isn't normal; it is *para*normal. *Meta*physical. *Peri*mortal. *Less* dense, not *more*. Let there be light. More light! The light shall set you free!

"If we are to discover any real truths about the paranormal, about near-death experiences, and about life after death, we will only do it if we stop taking everything so *seriously*," Moody counsels. "*Jay*-zus!" he says.

■   ■   ■

Thus granted license to open up to the playful paranormalism of porous worlds and multiple realities by none other than Raymond Moody, let us reapproach Lord Michael and his band of Rescue Angels.

These folks aren't new. By all accounts, they've been around forever. Dr. Carl and Anna Wickland say they worked with the Mercy Band in their psychic circles in the early 1900s. In fact, the Wimhurst machine Wickland used to shock discarnate spirits out of the bodies of his patients had been designed to angelic specifications—not unlike the technical assistance ITC continues to receive from spirit colleagues now.

"These are the Big Guns," said Laurel. "Archangel Michael is one of the Lords of Heaven. Jesus is a Lord of Heaven. Raphael, Gabriel—but Lord Michael is the Lord of Heaven whose responsibility it is to guard and protect everyone on this planet and to guide us safely to the other side. And, as I understand it, it's not like they are separate beings, but a large—*huge*—energy field."

"A field that has reached the Christ Energy level of consciousness," said Ruth. "Universal Wisdom, the essence of the Higher Power."

"I have a real strong faith that even if I should ask informally, 'Lord Michael, help this soul to the Light'—it's happening *now*!" Laurel clapped her hands.

"When the Higher Self of the individual that has the entities wants to be rid of them but the entities don't want to go, you call in Lord Michael and the rescue squad of angels and they will take the hitchhikers appropriately to the Light," said Ruth.

"And they can do that because you have brought them in—by request. The intercession of angels. Because of free will, they won't come in unless they are asked. It's always available to us, but they don't come unless they're asked."

So, Wally called in the Big Guns for the clearing of Lyle Hoop, and the dark force energies that had been attached to Lyle were swept away. The pendulum confirmed it. And again, for Sharon, the topless dancer. Wally asked, and it was done.

■   ■   ■

Molly's clearing was a little bit different. Earle Swenson's ex-wife, Molly, had grown aware of his presence shortly after his sudden death by heart attack at forty-five. They'd been divorced three years and Earle was living with his boyfriend, but he'd stayed in touch with Molly and still spent time with their son. There was love there. Also, there was anger and blame. And there were secrets.

With Earle's death, Molly had yet another reason to be mad at him. First, for leaving her after seventeen years of marriage, then for being gay (not, as he would have had it, bisexual), and now for being dead. She knew her anger wasn't rational and, as time went on, she would begin to work through it. But, in fact, Earle never really left. He had shown up at her house ten days after his funeral.

Molly woke to sounds in the middle of the night. She heard the basement door open and someone move into the hall. Molly found Earle standing in the bathroom, dressed in his suit coat and white shirt and tie but no underwear or pants or shoes or socks—just as his body had been dressed at the viewing before they closed the casket.

"He's either peeing in the sink or trying to use the sink and he doesn't remember what it's for," Molly told me. "And I look at him, and I say, 'What are you doing here?' and he said, 'Well, I don't think I live here anymore,' and I said, 'No, you don't live here.' And then I said, 'In fact, you're dead.' Later, somebody said to me, 'Well, did you tell him you loved him and he should go to the Light?' and I said 'No, I didn't want him in my house!'"

But Molly did want Earle in her house. And, from that night on, she continued to feel his presence. "I thought it was a good thing," she admitted. "I thought that meant he loved me, that he supported me, that he was like my angel, that he hadn't left."

He hadn't. He couldn't.

Several years later, after their boy had gone off to college and Molly no longer felt the anger and blame she'd suffered after the divorce and Earle's death, she began to feel like she wanted to get on with her life. She'd like to have some privacy for one thing. Maybe have a friend over to spend the night without having to think about Earle in the room. Molly also began to suspect that Earle himself would be better off if he got on with the business of being dead, whatever that entailed. She wasn't sure.

"I just told him he was dead. I didn't tell him what to do. I didn't know what to do." But she was suddenly convinced it wasn't right for him to be there.

It wasn't. There is no healthy upside to entity attachment, either for the entity or the host. Every possessing or obsessing spirit needs to be expelled.

But, Earle was stuck. He was being held back. What Ruth got from the pendulum was that Earle was being controlled by dark energy of some kind, that he knew full well he was dead and was willing to go to the Light—in fact, he wanted to go—but there was something preventing him.

"Dark energy fragments" is what the pendulum said.

"That Scandinavian gene pool," Molly told me. "All the scary things people do to each other during long winter nights." I felt a chill. "Like what?" I asked.

Earle's father's back had been covered with scars from being brutally beaten as a child. He never hit his boys. He simply froze them out; gave them nothing. Earle and his twin brother, who grew up to be a priest, had been sexually molested by a hired hand with the end of a pitchfork when they were very young. Repeatedly. And the twins had slept together in the same bed until well into their teens.

More than that remains a secret. And darkness persisted. And shame. The dark energy that prevented Earle from going to the Light had to first be cleared from Earle before Earle could be cleared from Molly.

"That was complicated for me," said Wally. "I drew myself some pictures so I could find out who was where and what's nested with what."

And then, Wally called on Lord Michael and the Mercy Band of Rescue Angels.

"And you don't have to ask them twice," said Ruth.

The dark energy was successfully cleared from Earle. Then, Earle was successfully cleared from Molly. "There was a release and a relief," Molly told me. "And that relief has been ongoing. My knowledge that he's no longer stuck has helped me not fall back into old patterns of anger and neediness. He still comes back once in awhile. Now I just say, 'Earle, go away.'" And he does. He can. He's not stuck.

Any more than the San Pedro mother is stuck. Or Charley Hoop. They can come back and visit. They can come and go.

We just won't let them stay. And, once a soul has made its true connection with the spirit world, they don't want to stay. There is too much going on for them there.

In the case of the entities that lived off Sharon, the attraction had not been love, devotion, or blood. It was alcohol and sex and drugs and tobacco and the high emotional drama of Sharon's chaotic life. People attract like vibrations to themselves. If Sharon doesn't choose to change how she lives her life, the addictive entities that were "picked off her like ticks from a dog," as her psychic mother saw it, and were carried to the Light by Lord Michael, will likely soon be replaced by others.

A lot of people don't want to participate in their own health care, to echo Ruth. You have to want to take that responsibility. Staying drunk, stoned, busted, broke, strung-out on negativity and hopelessness and victimhood is to relinquish that responsibility and to become a magnet for like vibrations from everywhere.

But, Earle's clearing worked. As had Molly's, and Lyle's, and Charley's, and Opal's. As have more than six hundred other hitchhiker clearings Wally and Ruth have done since before they stopped keeping track.

■   ■   ■

I have a question.

In the case of Marianne, the San Pedro mother who hitchhiked on her son, had she known that she was dead? She certainly knew she was dying. Her sick bed had been in the middle of the living room for five years. And, when I talked to her mother, Olivia, she said she'd had a strong intuition that her daughter had actually chosen the moment of her death.

"She told her father to take me home, 'Mom is tired,'" Olivia told me. "I said, 'But Tom isn't here yet,' and she said, 'He'll be coming.'

"To me, she cleared the scene for her death," Olivia told me. "She decided to go when she did."

Because, by the time Tom got there, she was gone.

"I think she had probably decided that once she had the stomach tube in, after surgery, and would have to be fed through a tube into the stomach, and it would have an exterior container—I think she just felt that it would be too much for Tom and the children."

Tom's care-giving skills were inadequate at best. He was angry at his wife for being sick in the first place, and his fear of being left to live without her manifested as resentment toward her parents' every effort to help, and as sporadic explosive rage against his children.

"Tom was going to put Marianne in a back bedroom where she couldn't see what was going on and it would be hard to take care of her and the room had mold in it," Olivia told me. "I said no. She has to be out where she's a part of the family and has some reason for being. And his response was, 'What for? She's not going to get well anyway.' And that just really hit me hard."

She had already cut back to three days a week and was trying to "stay out of their business," but she also tried to continue to protect the children. Gregory, the oldest, "seemed to understand things the others didn't and would hold his mother's hand and talk to her. The others didn't know what to do and Tom was no help. He couldn't handle it himself."

Olivia was there the day Tom went berserk because Gregory hadn't finished a chore he'd been assigned. Tom lit into him, kicking and screaming, "You're nothing but a piece of shit!"

"He just said it over and over and over," Olivia told me. We wondered out loud who had yelled at Tom like that.

She'd also been there the time Tom went ballistic and Greg had turned on him. "He had had it," said Olivia, "and he started kicking his dad, and Tom curled up on the floor in the fetal position and just let Gregory kick him and Gregory kept saying, 'I hate you, I hate you, I hate you.' He kept it up for quite a while, and finally, I sensed that he didn't know how to stop. I said, 'Greg, I think that's enough,' to calm him down. And he finally stopped."

Olivia had been there and been able to stop it. But, Marianne had also been there—flat on her back in the middle of the living room, hearing it all, unable to stop it, unable to swallow or to move.

So, had Marianne chosen to die when she did? And once dead, had she deliberately attached herself to Gregory in order to protect him in a way she'd been unable to during her bedridden, down-hill years?

Curiously enough, Gregory's clearing hadn't come about as the result of concerns about Gregory—though he had shut himself off, isolated and depressed since his mother's death—but because of feelings Olivia couldn't shake about Marianne.

"Right after she died, I thought someone had invaded the house. In the hallway there were three bookcases she had given us, and I felt something was not quite right. The bottom part of these bookcases opened by metal handles that were loose; they could flop back and forth. That's what I heard. That sound. We weren't in a very safe neighborhood, and I'm ashamed of myself for being afraid, but I didn't think of Marianne at the time. And I was so sorry because I felt like maybe I had disappointed her in that she had tried to reach me and I didn't understand, and, you know—if she was disappointed, then, why try again?"

Marianne never left Olivia's mind. "I never got to say goodbye," she said. "I hadn't heard from her all this time"—ten years—"and she's either not in a good place or she isn't happy or something," is what she told Ruth.

Ruth asked the pendulum. The pendulum said that Marianne had not crossed over. Had she attached to someone? Yes. Someone in the family? Yes. To Tom? No. To Gregory? Yes.

Whether by conscious design or vibrational attraction, Marianne's attachment to Gregory was strong, and she strongly resisted letting go.

Wally had gotten permission from Universal Intelligence to talk to Marianne's Higher Self. He didn't want to interfere and this was coming from love, he told her, but for the sake of Gregory's welfare and for the sake of her own, it would be healthier for her to let go and to go on with her path in life. She could always come back, he told her. She could visit. And Greg could always call on her if he ever needed help.

Reluctantly, Marianne finally agreed. She followed Wally's directions into the spirit world—sought the Light, called to loved ones—and left. The pendulum verified it. Marianne was gone.

"I felt great relief," Olivia told me. "And hoped that it was the right thing to do. I felt that it was, but I still had this feeling that maybe it wasn't my place to interfere with what was happening, and yet if somebody didn't . . ."

■　　■　　■

Bonnie Crate was a very large woman, square, built like a bumper car. She only had a few friends, and the friends she had were tired of her bullshit. "She's a bossy, opinionated control freak, very much on the 'pity pot,'" is what I was told. "There is nothing you can say that she won't put you down for or contradict or try to top you. She's a know-it-all. Her own daughter refuses to speak to her. And yet, she won't go anywhere. She's afraid to leave her house without her husband or someone. She's afraid to go outside."

When asked to find out if part of Bonnie's problem might not be spirit attachment, Ruth asked the pendulum and the pendulum said yes—four hitchhikers and four dark entities.

"Four and four," said Wally at the beginning of her clearing.

"I get that the hitchhikers are willing to go, but the entities will need help," said Ruth.

"Okay, now, using the pendulum we ask Universal Intelligence for permission to work with the Higher Self of Bonnie Crate. Do we have that permission?"

Yes.

"We request the presence and assistance of Lord Michael. Is Lord Michael present and willing to be of assistance?"

Yes.

"Thank you. Now we call into this bubble of light the Higher Self of Bonnie Crate and the hitchhikers and dark entities who are attached to her. Has Bonnie Crate's Higher Self and hitchhikers arrived in the circle of light?"

The pendulum said yes.

"Now, to the Higher Self of Bonnie Crate, do we have your permission to instruct the attached entities on how and why they should make a transition to the spirit world?"

This had never happened.

"I'm getting a no," said Ruth.

No?

"That's an interesting . . . development," said Ruth.

Wally doubled back.

"Let's ask the pendulum, how many discarnate spirits who have had a body, are in Bonnie Crate's energy system?"

"Four."

"And are three of them willing to go to the spirit world?"

"Actually, all four of them."

"All four are willing to go?"

"Bonnie seems to need to hang on . . ." Ruth trailed off.

"Bonnie doesn't want to let go?"

"Bonnie doesn't want to let go."

"Bonnie's Higher Self?"

"The Higher Self is willing to let *some* go, but there's a catch here," said Ruth. She asked the pendulum, "Willing to let go of one hitchhiker?"

The pendulum said yes.

"Two?"

Yes.

"Three?"

Yes.

"Four?"

No.

"Is the fourth hitchhiker a member of the family?"

Yes.

"Maybe it needs explaining to."

Wally launched into his script—You are in Bonnie Crate's body. It does not belong to you. Your body's dead. Research has shown. So much like being alive. Then something happened. Illness. Operation. You passed. Cord broke.

"Now—" said Wally when he'd finished, "Is this satisfactory for the one who did not want to leave?"

"I'm getting both yes and no and I think the problem is

that the entity understands and is willing to go but that Bonnie's Higher Self for some reason does not," said Ruth.

Wally gave exit instructions to the three hitchhikers who were willing to go and then asked Lord Michael to spirit off the dark ones to the Light. That done, he resumed:

"Let me ask the pendulum. We now have one hitchhiker that Bonnie Crate's Higher Self wants to stay with her. Is that correct?"

"Yes," said Ruth.

"One hitchhiker wants to stay?"

"Does the hitchhiker want to stay? No."

"The hitchhiker doesn't want to stay?"

"No."

"Well, the hitchhiker is a spirit. It has its own body. It has a spirit body."

"The hitchhiker is—"

"The spirit has a right," said Wally. "We ask Bonnie Crate's Higher Self to release its hitchhiker so that the hitchhiker can go to the spirit world where it can grow and learn as it should. The spirit body belongs in the spirit world, Bonnie. The spirit has a right."

This took more persuading, but the tape stops here. Someone turned it over. On the flip side, Wally wraps up his argument to Bonnie's Higher Self by saying that, complementary to Ruth's previous statement that we don't interfere with what the Higher Self wants, the soul of the entity also has rights—in this case, the right not to be prevented from getting on with it's life.

"Bonnie Crate's Higher Self, are you now willing to release this hitchhiker who appears to want to go to the spirit world and continue its growth?"

"She is willing," said Ruth.

"We instruct this entity to find a spot of light and to move toward that light and to call out to someone you know who is dead who cares about you . . . ."

Finishing up, Wally asked that the hitchhiker forgive Bonnie Crate for holding it so long, and asked Bonnie's Higher Self to forgive the hitchhikers and entities for everything they had done. He asked the members of the circle to project light and love into Bonnie's energy system in order to fill up the holes once occupied by the entities, then thanked Lord Michael and the angels, and shut off the tape recorder.

Later on, they resume:

"Okay, now, Ruth, this is different," Wally says on the tape.

"This is much different. I was saying that of the four hitchhikers I had determined that two were family and two were not. And that all of them had been in Bonnie's field for a long time."

"Like twenty years?"

"Ten years or more?" she asks the pendulum. "Yes. The one she did not want to let go, had that one been in her field for twenty years?"

Yes.

"For twenty-five years?"

Yes.

"For thirty years?"

Yes.

"Since childhood?"

"Since childhood," says Wally. "Was this an invisible friend?"

"No," says Ruth.

"Wasn't there at birth."

"Wasn't there at birth. Didn't come in with her."

"But came in in childhood."

"It was a family member to whom she was very attached as a child. That passed over. Was it a grandparent?"

"Grandparent, okay, died in Bonnie's childhood," says Wally.

"And who probably stayed to protect her?"

Yes.

"And then Bonnie wasn't willing to let her go. Or him. Grandfather?"

No.

"Grandmother," says Wally.

"But, I was saying that when I was holding the pendulum and you were asking questions, it was so obvious that there were some yeses and nos because first the pendulum would swing a yes and then it would immediately grab and swing a no. I can't make it do that. It was doing it just as though opposing forces were pulling at it. It couldn't *not* answer, but it couldn't stay with either answer because the strengths of the answers were so much the same."

■   ■   ■

"I can't make it do that," Ruth had said.

"What *can* you make it do?" I asked.

Her pendulum hung in the air. "Oh, I can make this answer any way I want it to answer, but . . ."

"You can override it?"

"Yes, and sometimes if I think that's what I'm doing, I'll just ask: Am I skewing this? And it will tell me. But, to be able to let go of outcome—that's what I mean by setting yourself aside. And, if it's something you're particularly invested in, then it's wise to ask. Also, if you only get answers you expect, then the chances are you are influencing it.

"But the thing that convinced Dr. Carol, particularly when we first started working, was that she could give me numbers and I had absolutely no notion of what they related to and it would still give accurate answers,' Ruth said.

"What *did* they relate to?" I asked.

"They were frequency settings, which I didn't know zilch about at the time, and she would say, 'Should we do nine seventy thirty-five?' And it would answer yes or no. There was no way I could have been influencing that because I didn't have a clue as to what any of it meant."

"So, that was Universal Knowledge answering—"

"No, I think that was my Higher Self. Although, you know—we are one." The Higher Self and Universal Knowledge. "We are one."

Here's her point.

"If the desire for truth is stronger than the ego, then you can let go of outcome. And in relation to questions about yourself, if you really want to *know* more than you want to be *right*, then you won't influence the pendulum."

It takes a long time. Ruth has been at this awhile.

"Her medical doctors say that there aren't many people that could pendle cancer in themselves and be trustworthy that they're not affecting the answers," said Wally. "But Ruth really wants to know."

■　　　■　　　■

The symptoms of spirit attachment are largely behavioral and psychological. Most clearings take place without the knowledge of the person attached and cleared, many times long distance. So, though "the proof is in the results," as Wally says, feedback about results is spotty.

We know Lyle went back to work feeling better, that he's been much more focused and not so confused.

We know Gregory finally came out of isolation. "He's got some girls chasing him, he's been going to parties," Olivia reported. At his new job there had been a lot of yelling and his coworkers asked him how he stayed so calm. "I don't feel calm inside," Gregory told his grandma, "but I told them I learned that from my grandma."

Bonnie Crate, for a while at least, was easier to live with, not so needy, less insistent on having her own way. She even ventured out of doors on her own.

"We cleared Faith," Ardis told me, "and I remember when we came home I asked Faith what she'd done the Sunday before and she said, 'You know, it's real strange, I was working around here and just being busy and then all of a sudden I just, about noon, I just felt really different.' And that was about the time that we had been working on her."

Anecdotal. Nothing science would accept. "You couldn't take it to court," Wally told me. Nope. No way to prove it. But proof is to focus on doubt. And doubt is a wall. And the world is made up of stories, not of atoms.

My own story goes like this.

■　　　■　　　■

Emaline Elizabeth ruled the roost. My great grandmother on my mother's side, matriarch of the Johnston clan, Emaline Elizabeth had her hand in everything. Her son, my grandpa, did his best to keep her happy, while his bride, my grandma, had the babies—ten in fourteen years. Emaline Elizabeth had gone with them on their honeymoon and lived in their house every day of their married life on a ragged string of farms up in Antelope County, Nebraska, until the day she died, when, according to the pendulum, she attached herself to Grandpa. When Grandpa died in 1943, Emaline Elizabeth jumped to her second son, my grandpa's brother, Harry.

Uncle Harry would lumber up our sidewalk through the lilac bushes wide as his shoulders—always wearing the same gray suit. Always parking his bullet-nosed Studebaker at the curb in the bleaching heat. The summer sun was butter and the sky was white and the emerald trees above us heaved in very slow motion. One huge ham hand would come out to me in the shade of the porch and we would silently shake. He'd nod. Mom opened the screen door behind me and Harry'd go in. He had typing for Mom. The two of them were close.

As close as Mom had been to her first boss, Professor Schwenk, in Agronomy. "I made twenty-five cents an hour," she told us many times. "I took dictation by hand. It was the Depression. I had no choice. The family needed money. I would have liked to gone to college, but I couldn't go to college because the family needed money" and she never owned a bicycle of her own till she was forty.

Back in Naples, Florida, when Ruth and Wally started doing clearings, they asked and got the answer that Norene, my mom, had five hitchhikers—two unidentified males, my father Roscoe, Professor Schwenk, and Uncle Harry. So, they cleared her. And she seemed okay. But gradually she grew more negative. She gained weight, "lost her quads"—the use of her quadriceps femoris (thigh) muscles—and, somewhere along the line, she threw a clot and wound up in Intensive Care.

Ruth probably saved her life.

"When she had the emboli," Ruth said, "I don't think there's any question but that TT kept her alive. The doctor didn't expect her to live." Ruth worked through the night. "I didn't care whether they thought I was crazy or not, and when a doctor'd come in, I'd step out and when they'd move out, I'd move back in and do TT. When I wasn't working on her, I was *visualizing* working on her."

Mom survived. And after several months in rehab, she returned to the apartment where she lived alone, sat down in the motorized, tilting chair that Ruth had had delivered, turned on the Weather Channel, and steadily grew even more depressed.

That summer her depression was finally eclipsed by my own. When I came through that time, I simply had no patience with her. I wanted to throw her down the steps. Instead, and likely because of my own agitation, according to the pendulum, I attracted Mom's remaining hitchhiker—Emaline Elizabeth. She had been nested with Uncle Harry. Nobody knew she was there. When Harry went to the Light, she stayed with Mom. Now, for the worst part of what became a miserable year, Emaline Elizabeth piggy-backed on me.

Ruth and Laurel came down from Seattle to Wally and Ardis's place. I was in New York, not thinking about it, when this *whoa!*—just this—*release*—happened. In my chest, my upper arms, this—light. My crown chakra literally lifted toward the ceiling, and the ceiling lifted, and my spine straightened and the fluid in it cooled, and a profound weight just—went.

Emaline Elizabeth was gone.

My time (Eastern) was around four o'clock in the afternoon.

Their time (Pacific) was around one o'clock in the afternoon.

Same time, no time, same field.

There is only the present.

13

And What to Do about It

WE'RE LIKE TWO FARMERS BITING WHEAT, standing in the field, eyes on the horizon.

"Nothing you could take to court," said Wally.

"Definitely anecdotal," I agree. "Radical empiricism," I invoke William James.

"Can't prove a thing."

"Can't prove a thing."

"And if proof is required—" Wally begins.

"You can't have enough proof," I finish.

"Thelma Moss knew a nun who had a rose in her dresser drawer that was in full bloom and had been for twenty-two years."

"*Jay*-zus!" I quote Raymond Moody.

"And people said, 'How did she do that?' And Thelma just giggled and said, 'I don't know, I just have fun.'"

"I don't know, I just have fun," I repeat.

Wally pauses.

"I don't have to know that these clearings are successful."

I turn toward him.

"It's not going to make any difference if this didn't change anything for any spirit," he says. "Or, if there *aren't* any spirits."

Wally's pretty sure there are. He knows that when what looks like spirit attachment is treated as if that's what it is, symptoms disappear. Depressions lift, self-destructive behavior stops, energy returns. Both possessed and possessor seem freed to get on with the business of living their lives and so-called deaths.

It can be dangerous. Suicidal spirits can latch onto living humans beings and try to kill themselves—repeatedly. The souls of the addicted dead will drive their hosts to extremes of substance abuse and self-abuse and abuse of others. Even well-meaning entities may damage those they think they are protecting because neither one's aware of what the bleep is going on.

Souls lost in the darkness and confusion of not knowing they are dead, or what death is, or what to do about it, can get ornery. Some get ugly, others bully. Some become belligerent SOBs.

Every possessing entity needs to be expelled.

How?
First, get their attention.
Then, tell them the truth.
The truth may be that the one possessed has had a part in drawing the possessor to them.
Man is an open system, an energetic field, coextensive with the universe, continuously exchanging matter and energy with the environment, according to Martha Rogers.
E equals mc squared. Matter and energy are the same thing. Everything is energy. Everything vibrates.

"Whether energy expresses itself as physical or nonphysical is a matter of the speed at which molecules vibrate." (Robert Williams, *Psych K: The Missing Peace in Your Life*) This is what I was getting at when I quoted Drunvalo in chapter seven. It's what George Meek told Mark Macy back in 1991.

"Mind is simply molecules of YOU vibrating at a higher rate than the body molecules of YOU." (Williams, *Psych K*)

The body/mind connection heralded by the New Age is, finally, the recognition that, while our brain is a physical mass of billions of cells cradled in our skulls, our mind is *an energy field that interpenetrates and surrounds it.* In fact, our minds may surround our entire body and extend—how far out? How far beyond the physical body do our energy bodies go? How far beyond the physical body do our conscious minds extend? How many minds are there?

"The sum total of all the minds in the universe is one." (Erwin Schrodinger)

Does that mean "we are one" is literal truth? Is this the end of us and them? Of black and white? Of good and evil? Might this mean that all of us contain a spark of the divine, a flicker of God-consciousness?

If so, it might behoove us to treat one another as we would like to be treated if we, too, were a lost soul—firmly, but with kindness. Certainly with the recognition that we may have had a hand in whatever spiritual interference we experience.

"People on earth draw into their lives spirit beings of like attitude."

This is good news. If we can take responsibility for our part in the process, we may be able to change the reality of our lives and free ourselves from the fear of lions.

When I was young it was the Russians, the bomb. I "ducked

and covered" I don't know how many years. In fact, the world has been a fearsome place from conception. Every fear my mother had, every worry she worried, effervesced in my bloodstream. Her chemistry was mine. Everything heard, every feeling felt before I was "me," before I was conscious, certainly before I was conscious of being me—and who can tell us when the soul actually enters the body without quoting Scripture? Everything comes as stimulus/response, as protein behavior, from when we're still inside our mothers. Experiences "from the moment of conception are creating memories, receptors, and programmed responses," long before we are able to discern what's going on. (Lipton, *The Biology of Perception, the Psychology of Change*)

Then, after we are born, the environment takes over, shaping beliefs about what is and isn't real and where the dangers lie.

But must we suffer consensus fears such that we shut down our immune systems? Become so negative that we draw into our vibrating auras the confused, depressed, addicted spirit entities that swirl in clouds above our magic planet?

Rob Williams says we can change our beliefs (hence the beings we attract)—if we know which mind to talk to.

He points to three.

The *conscious mind* is volitional, sets goals and judges results, thinks abstractly, and likes new, creative ideas. Time-bound, it is focused on the past and future. Its short-term memory is twenty seconds long. Processing an average of two thousand bits of information per second, it can't do more than a few things at once.

The *subconscious mind* is habitual and monitors all operations of the body including motor functions, heart rate, respiration, and digestion. It thinks literally and only knows the world through the senses. It focuses exclusively in present time and uses past learning to perform habitual functions like walking, talking, and driving a car. It can do thousands of jobs at once because it processes four billion bits of information per second-as long as the information is literal, perceived through the senses and experienced in the present.

The subconscious mind also stores our memories and beliefs. According to Williams, this is the mind we need to talk to if we want to change. But, it is called *sub*conscious for a reason. We can't speak directly to it. It does not pick up messages or return calls. We are unconscious of the bulk of the beliefs it holds.

The *superconscious mind*, on the other hand, is a part of consciousness *beyond both our conscious and subconscious minds*. It serves as a bridge between them and monitors their evolutionary progress toward what Williams calls their "eventual unification or oneness." He calls this superconscious mind the Higher Self and says it connects to Universal Knowledge.

Ruth and Wally believe that the pendulum taps into Universal Knowledge. "It is consciousness in the broadest sense," Ruth said. "If you don't get in its way and maybe if you believe it, kinesiology and dowsing and the pendulum" are the same.

Kinesiology, or muscle testing, is how Rob Williams has learned to communicate with the subconscious mind. Habitual, literal, the monitor of body functions, knowing what it knows only through the senses—the subconscious mind can be reached through the sense of touch, through the muscles. Williams does it through the deltoid muscle.

Stand to one side of your partner, face each other looking over the other's shoulder. Person being tested holds their arm out to the side parallel to the floor. Tester rests one hand lightly on the wrist of the person being tested, the other hand on his/her shoulder. Person being tested keeps his/her body relaxed, face forward, eyes open, focused down, chin parallel to the floor. Then makes a statement.

Tester says "be strong" and applies a gentle, steady pressure in a downward direction at the wrist. Person being tested resists the pressure of the downward motion and their deltoid muscle either locks in or lets go. Strong means true or yes. Weak means false or no.

Try it.

It works.

Our bodies know the truth. Through muscle testing and the pendulum we can access our unconscious attitudes and beliefs through the subconscious mind, which connects to the field of universal knowledge through the Higher Self.

We are not victims. Of our genes, of our perceptions, or of our beliefs. Nor are all of the experts "out there" somewhere. The force that moves the pendulum is not outside the body. The force that moves the pendulum is the field. We are part of that field. We have access to that knowledge. We can ask questions and get answers. We can listen. We can learn.

> Human minds [are] connected to each other, just as they [are] connected to everything else in this world and every other world. (McTaggart, *The Field*)

■   ■   ■

Sections of Wally's script for clearing hitchhiker spirits appear throughout this book. Wally nixed my idea to print the full text as an appendix. "It'll be cookbookish," he said. "The how-to part, I think, would be premature. This is the way *we* do it. This doesn't mean that this is how *you* do it. You have to be flexible. If they want something like that"—a recipe—"they've got it in Edith Fiore's book."

So, what to do about spirit attachment?

First, get their attention. Carl Wickland did this with enough electrical current to drive the spirits from his patients into the body of his wife. Edith Fiore does it through hypnotic trance. Bill Baldwin called it an altered state.

When they clear at a distance, Ruth and Wally ask Universal Knowledge for permission to speak to the Higher Self of the person who is attached. They then ask that person's Higher Self for permission to instruct the attached entity or entities on how and why they should make a transition to the spirit world.

If the Higher Self says yes, they tell the spirit the truth:

You are not (possessed's name).
Your body is dead.
You joined (possessed's name).
You are harming yourself and (possessed's name).
Your loved ones are here.
You will be in a perfect body.
There is no such thing as hell.
You will have a wonderful, peaceful life.
Go in peace and with my blessings.

This is boilerplate from Fiore's *The Unquiet Dead*, which is where Ruth and Wally started. Since then, they've learned to be flexible and improvise. If things get complicated, Wally may draw a stick figure diagram of who is who. He'll tack left, he'll tack right. Through their combined understanding of human psychology, he and Ruth are able to tune into "the feeling tone," to listen for "the healthy part" of the entities they deal with, to be present, stay in the moment, and remember—*you can do no harm.*

"You can do no harm" is a guiding principle of TT, Healing Touch, Jin Shin Jyutsu, and other energy healing disciplines. The understanding is that healing energy will always flow to where it is needed in the body—even if you don't always get your fingers exactly where they belong. Something like that also seems to work when releasing earthbound spirits. And, if you do get into trouble, you can always call Lord Michael.

So, what do you do if it is *you* who are attached?

First, realize that "there's always some sort of an invitation at some level," says Wally. "Even if it's just your ignorance of it that allows it to happen. The host person should be able to control it because they've got dibs on the body. You know, 'It's my body. *Out!*' You're not a hapless victim. It's not a terrorizing thing. It's your body and you can take charge better than they can."

Online at *www.alchemicalmage.com*, under Tools and Techniques, there appears a procedure called Entity Release, which comes from the *Tools for Living Heaven* tape set. Designed to clear human energy fields of astral entities, negative thought-forms and emotions, dark forces, parasites, and the ubiquitous boogie, the release is described as "a good practice in any Spiritual Hygiene program." It is a way to take charge.

I quote:

Many times, astral entities will intrude on our fields. Whether conscious or unconscious, we make agreements with them when we have moments of fear or need. These entities will attach themselves to us, usually promising some aspect of ourselves comfort in exchange for living vicariously through us. These exchanges are almost never worth it, as the astral entity is just as subject to distortion and the illusion of polarity as are beings of the Third Dimension. They often feed on addictions of various types, be they for substances or people. Some really enjoy anger and violence and will spur arguments and feed off karmic situations, adding to the intensity of the karma. Sometimes, relationships between people are actually relationships between the entities attached to them! It is always of benefit to release these beings into the Light, so that they can move on to their next stage of development and you can be free of their influence. Some people do the Entity Release on a regular basis, just to be sure no entities have "sneaked" into their fields.

Entity Release

Call for assistance: "Archangel Michael please bring down the tunnel of Light. Ariel, Azrael, and Aru-Kiri, please assist.

"I break any and all agreements or contracts, both conscious and unconscious, that I have made, anyone in my body has made, or anyone in my genetic lineage has made, with any astral entities, negative thought-forms or emotions, demons, dark forces or boogies. Please go into the tunnel, we will take you home."

From the moment you begin an entity release, assume that feelings or thoughts may not be your own. Boredom, spaciness, resistance, "this stuff never works," anger, aches and pains, and grief may all be coming from entities. Identify them and send them on, i.e.

"Entity holding resistance: go into the Light!" Toning is very helpful to ease their release. When you feel clear or lighter, ask Michael to take the tunnel back to the Fifth Dimension.

The last time Wally and I worked on this manuscript together, he'd just discovered David Hawkins's book *Power vs. Force*. He thinks it may be something Ruth knew about, but it hadn't registered with him until he found it on the Internet while looking for something else. Hawkins's work plugs right into Bruce Lipton and Rob Williams, and that has gotten Wally going. His cerebral corn pops.

Here's what Wally has written about Hawkins:

The Purpose of Life

The purpose of life is to learn and develop our potential. This is the process of human development. Without the spirit we would not be human, so human development includes spiritual development. The ultimate goal in spiritual development is enlightenment. So, how do we get there? How do we grow spiritually? How can we achieve our purpose in life?

In *Power vs. Force*, David Hawkins describes the steps on the logarithmic scale that lead to enlightenment. Hawkins identifies the 17 steps or levels on his "Map of Consciousness" from the least spiritual to the most spiritual. The levels are: Shame, Guilt, Apathy, Grief, Fear, Desire, Anger, Pride, Courage, Neutrality, Willingness, Acceptance, Reason, Love, Joy, Peace, and Enlightenment.

The optimist and the pessimist live in very different worlds. The world that we each *experience* depends upon our unique *perceptions* of the world. Those perceptions are determined by our individual belief systems, what we believe about ourselves, others, society, life, liberals, conservatives, the world, God, the hereafter, etc.

To develop spiritually, we must move from one level to the next, step by step up the ladder. To do that requires a change in our beliefs. Fortunately, we can identify and examine our beliefs. We can create new ones, or borrow from quotations that have stood the test of time. Using Hawkins's technique, which involves Applied Kinesiology, we can calibrate the "truth-level" of all the beliefs in the pool and choose those that will advance our spiritual development the most.

Beliefs are stored in the subconscious mind. They operate automatically and are very difficult to change with the conscious mind by using such techniques as affirmations and resolutions. In their videotape, *The Biology of Perception, The Psychology of Change*, Bruce Lipton and Rob Williams describe a rapid method of changing beliefs, especially those that have been holding us back.

David Hawkins's "Map of Consciousness" describes the ladder to spiritual growth. The work of Lipton and Williams describes how to negotiate those steps deliberately, intelligently and rapidly. It appears that rapid spiritual growth is now possible. Advancement in fulfilling the purpose in life is available. Could there by any activity more vital or satisfying? What are we waiting for?

—WALLY JOHNSTON,
OCTOBER 2004

■   ■   ■

Like two farmers biting wheat, standing in the field, eyes on the horizon.

"Man is made of belief," Wally says. "As he believes, so he is."

"The Bhagavad Gita," I say.

"As quoted by Aldous Huxley in *The Perennial Philosophy*, page 179."

"The paranormal is nonsense from nowhere."

Wally blinks. "Is that Moody?"

"*Jay*-zus!" I confirm.

Wally pauses.

"I don't have to know that these clearings are successful."

I turn toward him.

"It's not going to make any difference if this didn't change anything for any spirit," he says. "Or, if there *aren't* any spirits."

A delicate blue with golden light seems to come from everywhere.

"I'd be hard to convince at this point that there isn't an afterlife. Because I've been exposed to so much of it. Including with Michael."

Which is where we came in.

14

Where We Came In

MICHAEL BERRY JOHNSTON
NOVEMBER 15, 1957–MARCH 24, 1965

MICHAEL BERRY JOHNSTON KNEW HE WAS DEAD. The last time he came through was in 1981.

"It was about midnight," Ardis told me. "They were at our house and we were getting ready to go to bed and Vic looked at Lorraine and he says, 'Is that Michael over there?' She immediately went into trance and brought Michael through. He said, 'I just wanted you to know that I'm going to be moving on.' And so I said, 'How do you know when it's time to move on? Is it verbal or otherwise?' He says, 'No, it's just a feeling we get.'

"So then I asked him if he knew about Jerry's accident, and he says, 'Oh yes.'"

Michael's older brother, Jerry, was behind the wheel of an eighteen-wheeler coming down Mount Hood when his brakes failed. A trooper holding traffic at the construction site where an escape ramp was being built turned a radar gun on Jerry. He had him clocked doing eighty-two when he crashed. Jerry's right front wheel hit a front-end loader. His left rear dual drivers hit the dump truck, and the scoop dumping rocks sheered off the top of his cab. It took an hour and a half to cut him out of the wreckage. He had four shattered teeth and the design of the steering wheel printed in his belly. Chained to the trailer he'd been pulling was a Caterpillar bulldozer that had three claws to tear up concrete. One of the claws had somehow held to the splintered flatbed planking. Otherwise, Jerry would be dead.

Yes, Michael knew.

"He says, 'I was working with a group of children at the time and all of a sudden, I felt this pull,'" Ardis said. "'And I didn't know whether I should leave the children or not, but I had seen others leave their groups.' So he was pulled to Jerry's accident and he said, 'He's not ready to talk to me yet. But I was there.'

"And now I asked him if he was aware of my brother's death. My brother Don had died in 1981, and he says, 'Yes, but Uncle Don isn't ready to talk to me either.' I imagine he was sleeping because with his Methodist upbringing he probably thought that his reward was just to go to sleep forever, you know. And I asked about my dad, who had died in '71, and he says, 'Oh, Grandpa is just having a ball.' He says, 'He greets people that come over and he says, 'You don't need that wooden leg anymore, you don't need that cane.' And I can see him doing that, 'cause he loved people.

"And then I guess that was about the extent of it, wasn't it?"

Wally nodded. They're not sure. They hadn't gotten that one on tape.

The last time they'd been able to tape record Michael "was the night that Vic and Lorraine came to the door and Wally was still teaching in Rochester, and Lorraine was trying to hold off her trance until Wally got home," Ardis said. "The interesting thing was that when they first came to the door, the breezeway light wouldn't turn on, and I thought, there's four bulbs up there, I said, I never heard of four bulbs burning out at the same time, but we just went on and visited."

Lorraine finally couldn't hold off her trance any longer, and "Vic had brought his tape recorder but no microphone, so I hooked up one of Wally's microphones and she went into trance and Michael came through.

"It's interesting that Julie [their youngest], having never known Michael because she was born three years after he was killed, would be able to feel his energy beside her bed at night when she was very young. And then she told us one time that Michael was helping her with her arithmetic at school, giving her answers, and we kind of looked at her 'cause that's when Vic and Lorraine were coming over and we thought, well, she just wants to get into the act.

"But Michael says, 'Yes, Julie, I was helping you with the answers, but I realize now that you have to do it on your own. I can't be around all the time.'

"Then he said, 'Jer'—Jerry was there 'cause he says—'Jer, you've got your head on straight. Keep it that way, 'cause I'm watching.'

"Well, Wally comes home at eleven o'clock and we're going to play this tape back to him and it didn't work. So Wally said to Lorraine, can you bring him through again? And she says, 'Well, I've never done this before but I'll try.' So she laid down, went into trance, and when he came through Michael says, 'Well, you better get it right this time because I have things to do!'"

We laughed.

"It was interesting that Jerry came over that late at night and said 'I don't know why I'm here,'" said Wally.

"He stood out in the kitchen, leaning against the sink looking out the window the whole time Lorraine was in trance," Ardis said. "He came back the next day and he says, 'Mom, what do you think about that tape that she did last night?' and I said, 'Well, Jerry, I'm still looking for any clue that she might have previous knowledge, but . . .'

"'Well, I don't know why I came over at a quarter to eleven at night,' Jerry said. He'd never done that before."

"The breezeway light the next day," Wally added. "There's four bulbs up there and one of them was already burned out. The other three worked again the next day."

"Vic and Lorraine said that when they came to the door that night, they knew that Michael was going to come through," said Ardis, "and so they were pretty sure that it was Michael that turned the lights off."

"Michael was pushing," said Wally.

"He was putting Lorraine to sleep before she wanted to go to sleep."

"She tried to hold it off—'Stay awake, stay awake in this reality,' Wally continued. "Well, see, her first experience with Michael was he charged right in. He took over."

Michael was instrumental in the path that Wally and Ardis have taken in their lives.

"Definitely," said Ardis. "We were told by a psychic in '77 in Novato that Michael came to get us on the right path. She said that if he had stayed around he would have been very—what word did she use? Discontent or . . ."

"A bored misfit, probably," said Wally.

"That made it easier," said Ardis. "To accept."

And about the hitchhiker clearings? About their work with Ruth releasing earthbound spirits?

"I believe that works because I believe in the pendulum," said Wally. "And I believe in the pendulum because Ruth is still alive."

15

The Next Little While

IN MAY OF 2003, RUTH FLEW THREE THOUSAND some odd miles from Seattle to an island off the coast of North Carolina to be present at the wedding of my son and his wife.

A month before that, another oncologist had rendered yet another sentence. He gave Ruth three months to live.

We're at a beach house on stilts. There are fourteen wooden steps to the sand. A sliding glass door opens onto a porch overlooking the Atlantic. The waves come in, the waves go out, the waves come in. Pelicans fly by. Ruth is racked back in the living room recliner.

"I had a heart-to-heart with my pendulum, did I tell you?"

No, she hadn't.

"I don't know whether it thought I couldn't handle the truth or where it thinks it gets its authorization, but it told me that the CA 27/29 was coming down and when the tests came back, it had doubled. So, I thought 'Now, you little bugger.'"

"What were your numbers?"

"It wouldn't tell me the numbers. It was hedging. You know, easing me into it. Apparently, I still had to be in a bit of denial—not about the cancer, but about the extent to which it had blown up."

"What *are* the numbers?"

"My CA 27/29 went from eighty-two—which was at the time that I had the PET scan—eighty-two to four eleven. To eleven hundred. To twenty-two something."

"Ruth. What's the bone scan say? What's the CT scan?"

"It's a little grim. There's metastasis in several areas. My work is cut out for me. It's a bit of a shock. We'll handle it. At least the pendulum is telling me straight now."

"How do you know that?"

Several nights before she'd had excruciating pain in her liver—couldn't eat, couldn't sleep, finally at five o'clock in the morning, Ruth asked her pendulum: Is this a message? And it swung wide, yes. "And if I get to understand the message, will the pain go away?" It said yes.

"And so I started interviewing my liver," she said.

Earlier, the pendulum had said okay to a medication Dr. Wright prescribed for another condition. It was being overnighted, so Ruth hadn't begun to take it, but she'd started on the diet the medicine required.

Her liver told her that the diet was absolutely wrong. She shouldn't take the medication.

"I asked, as I do all the way along now, will this increase my chances of survival if I do *not* do this? Yes it will. So, I agreed."

Through the pendulum, she got the answers she needed. It told her to drink some hot water and apply external heat. Within an hour, she had no pain.

"I haven't had any liver pain since."

"One drawback with the pendulum, it'll only answer what you ask it. You've got to educate your intuition to ask the right questions. I got in trouble with the microcurrent because I was asking 'Do I need this?' Well, yeah, I need it. But, what I should have asked was 'Can I tolerate this?' Because I couldn't. I over-did. It's tricky, the subtleties. It's very specific."

"You were in denial."

"We were sneaking up on the seriousness of it. That's a little hard to continue to do when somebody sits there and says, 'Now, with a liver like yours the usual course is three months or less.' According to him, the only chance I've got is low-dose chemo. I said no. To me, that's Russian roulette. I know what that course is. But I don't know for sure what microcurrent will do or some of these other things I'm trying. Again, it's cutting edge, it's all uncharted waters, but there's an herb which has shown to be helpful with malaria and somehow somebody serendipitously discovered—at least in test tubes—that it will kill cancer cells.

"Sometimes people ask if I'm not concerned that some-thing isn't FDA approved. I think I'd be more concerned if it was anymore.

"At least the pendulum is telling me straight now."

"What is it saying?"

"My chances of survival are better this week than they were last week. Slim, but, you know, the odds can be against you. You don't need them all anyway."

"The odds can be against you, you don't need them all anyway?"

"You can have a ninety percent chance, you can have a ten percent chance, you can have a five percent chance. As long as you've got a chance."

She gazes out the window. Something else is on her mind.

"What's hard is if you're surrounded by people that don't believe, because you run out of energy. You need your energy to believe and to move forward. And if you have all these people creating doubt along the way and you have to ward all that off, it takes too much of your energy.

"I'm not going to live my life in fear. Most people do. Most health care situations are managed in fear. That's the way they handle it. They scare the bejesus out of people."

She looks directly at me.

"I am not an addled old woman."

"Who said you were?"

"It was *their* fear. *They* were afraid. But I felt like I was being cross-examined, interrogated, almost implying that I wasn't able to think clearly about what was going on. It was as though all my life-the assumption was that all of these decisions were flaky decisions out of nowhere. Every one of the things I am doing is research based. It may be research that's not yet published. It may be research that's not yet fully clinically trialed, but it's all research."

"Experts told you sixteen years ago you wouldn't live two years."

"That's right."

"That's sixteen years of research you have done on yourself."

"And nothing contradicts. Neither Wally nor I has run up against anything that really—'If you believe this, then this has got to be wrong.' It's not like that. It's as though—well, Wally talks about the Cosmic Jigsaw Puzzle. Every time we get another piece, and it fits, then something else makes sense. Everything connects."

The same three months about which her new oncologist was saying, "This is the usual pattern," Dr. Carol was saying, "This is a crucial time for us to get this thing under control."

"We can't mess around," said Ruth. "We've got this much time. It's going to slow down and gradually turn around. We should—within the next little while—begin to see at first a slowing down in terms of the lab reports, and then a reversal of the abnormality."

"You're not afraid of death," I said.

"Not really."

"Neither is Wally. He says, 'There's no such thing as death. And this is not the real world.'"

"You know, for me, it's funny 'cause a lot of people have to have a lot of answers. The whole thing for me really rests with the principle of physics. As far as what happens next—not what happens next, but the fact that there *is* a next—is the fact that we are energy and energy is never lost. It merely changes form. That to me is sufficient. I am perfectly comfortable with the ambiguity of not knowing what form it's going to take, and there are lots of ideas and lots of theories out there. It's totally separate from the notion of reincarnation. You don't have to believe in reincarnation to believe that life goes on."

"No, but you have to believe that consciousness slash mind slash soul . . ."

"Consciousness *is*."

"Well, consciousness is. Yes. But, the survival of our personality is still in question. You can't destroy energy, but can you destroy personality? Is there survival of personality?"

"That has never troubled me that much because whether it exists in an individualized form or not, the impact, the influence, the parts of us that are part of the people who come along after and who come along after and who come along after, can't be denied."

"It can't be denied in *this* dimension. There is evidence for it here. But is there survival of individual consciousness? I know, the whole thing is consciousness. It is one conscious field. But is there survival of individual consciousness within that field?"

"See, that to me is not important."

"Well. Good."

"Because, if we are one, how individual does it need to be?"

"Memories. I guess I'm talking about the survival of memories."

"The collective unconscious. I think Jung had an idea there that was way beyond what he knew he had. And when you stop and think about the Christ Energy, for instance, and the different manifestations of that Christ Energy, whether it's in the form of Buddha or Christ or Lord Michael—that level of being exists. And it manifests depending on what the needs are at a given time. Some manifestation comes forth as it is needed."

"That frequency of vibration exists."

"It does."

"That frequency of vibration—that's what I want to know about. I want to know how that works."

"And you will."

Four pelicans fly by.

■   ■   ■

"When anybody said to me, 'You need to write a book,' I said no, I don't need to write a book," Ruth said. "If the book is going to be written, Gary can write it and I'll talk to him."

Thanks for talking to me. Both of you. All of you. I love you.

■   ■   ■

"If we are one, how individual does it need to be?"

Ruth L. Johnston
February 2, 1927–June 17, 2003

Bibliography and Suggested Reading

Allison, Ralph, M.D. with Ted Schwarz. *Mind in Many Pieces*. New York: Rawson, Wade, 1980.

Baldwin, William J. *CE-VI: Close Encounters of the Possession Kind*. Terra Alta, WV: Headline Books, Inc., 1999.

———. *Healing Lost Souls*. Charlottesville, VA: Hampton Roads, 2003.

———. *Spirit Releasement Therapy*. Falls Church, VA: Human Potential Foundation Press, 1992.

Bentov, Itzhak. *A Brief Tour of Higher Consciousness*. Rochester, VT: Destiny Books, 2000.

———. *Stalking the Wild Pendulum*. Rochester, VT: Destiny Books, 1988.

Bird, Christopher. *The Divining Hand: The 500-Year-Old Mystery of Dowsing*. Atglen, PA: Whitford Press, 1993.

Castaneda, Carlos. *The Teachings of Don Juan: A Yaqui Way of Knowledge*. New York: Simon and Schuster, 1968.

Chaplin, Annabel. *The Bright Light of Death*. Marina del Ray, CA: DeVorss, 1977.

Crabtree, Adam. *Multiple Man: Explorations in Possession and Multiple Personality*. Toronto: Collins, 1985.

Crabtree, Adam. *Zero Trance: The Psychology of Maximum Experience*. New York: St. Martin's, 1997.

Ferguson, Marilyn. *The Aquarian Conspiracy*. Los Angeles: J.P. Tarcher, 1980.

Fiore, Edith. *The Unquiet Dead*. New York: Ballantine Books, 1988.

———. *You Have Been Here Before*. New York: Ballantine Books, 1978.

Frissell, Bob. *Nothing in This Book Is True, But It's Exactly How Things Are*. Berkeley: Frog, Ltd., 1994.

———. *Something in This Book Is True*. Berkeley: Frog, Ltd., 1997.

———. *You Are a Spiritual Being Having a Human Experience*. Berkeley: Frog, Ltd., 2001.

Green, Elmer. *The Ozawkie Book of the Dead*. Los Angeles: Philosophical Research Society, 2001.

Green, Elmer and Alyce Green. *Beyond Biofeedback*. New York: Dell Publishing, 1977.

Harman, Willis and Howard Rheingold. *Higher Creativity*. Los Angeles: J.P. Tarcher, 1984.

Hawkins, David. *Power vs. Force*. Carlsbad, CA: Hay House, Inc., 2002.

———. *The Eye of the I: From Which Nothing Is Hidden*. Sedona, AZ: Veritas Publishing, 2001.

Head, Joseph and S.L. Cranston, compilers and editors. *Reincarnation: The Phoenix Fire Mystery*. New York: Julian Press/Crown, 1977.

Hunt, Dr. Valerie. *Infinite Mind: Science of the Human Vibrations of Consciousness*. Malibu: Malibu Publishing, Co., 1996.

Huxley, Aldous. *Brave New World*. New York: Perennial, 1969.

———. *The Doors of Perception*. New York: Harper and Row, 1954.

———. *The Perennial Philosophy*. New York: Harper and Row, 1944.

Ireland-Frey, Louise. *Freeing the Captives*. Charlottesville, VA: Hampton Roads, 1999.

Johnston, W.W. *Take Charge! A Guide to Feeling Good*. Portland, OR: Acorn Endeavors, 1986.

Keyes, Daniel. *The Minds of Billy Milligan*. New York: Random House, 1981.

Kubis, Dr. Pat and Mark H. Macy. *Conversations Beyond the Light*. Boulder, CO: Griffin Publishing, 1995.

Kubler-Ross, Elisabeth. *Death: The Final Stage of Growth*. Englewood Cliffs, NJ: Prentice-Hall, 1975.

———. *On Death and Dying*. New York: Colliers McMillan, 1969.

———. *The Wheel of Life*. New York: Scribner, 1997.

Lipton, Bruce and Robert M. Williams. *The Biology of Perception, the Psychology of Change*, videotape, www.Psych-K.com.

Macy, Mark. *Conversations Beyond the Light: Communication with Departed Friends and Colleagues by Electronic Means*. Griffin Publishing, 1995.

———. *Miracles in the Storm*. New York: Penguin Putnam, 2001.

Maurey, Eugene. *Exorcism: How to Clear at a Distance a Spirit Possessed Person*. Westchester, PA: Whitford Press, 1988.

McTaggart, Lynne. *The Field*. New York: Harper Collins, 2002.

Meek, George W. *After We Die, What Then?* Columbus, OH: Ariel Press, 1987.

Melchizedek, Drunvalo. *The Ancient Secret of the Flower of Life*. Flagstaff, AZ: Light Technology Publishing, vol. 1, 1998, vol. 2, 2000.

Milanovich, Dr. Norma, and Dr. Shirley McCune. *The Light Shall Set You Free*. Albuquerque, NM: Athena, 1996.

Monroe, Robert A. *Far Journeys*. Garden City, NY: Doubleday, 1985.

———. *Journeys Out of the Body*. Garden City, NY: Doubleday, 1971.

———. *Ultimate Journey*. New York: Doubleday, 1994.

Moody, Raymond A. *The Last Laugh*. Charlottesville, VA: Hampton Roads, 1999.

———. *Life After Life*. New York: Bantam Books, 1976.

Moody, Raymond A. with Paul Perry. *Reunions: Visionary Encounters with Departed Loved Ones*. New York: Ivy Books, 1993.

Netherton, Morris and Nancy Schiffrin. *Past Lives Therapy*. New York: William Morrow, 1978.

Powell, A.E. *The Astral Body*. Wheaton, IL: Quest Books, 1996.

Raudive, Konstantin. *Breakthrough*. New York: Taplinger Publishing Co., 1971.

Ritchie, George G. with Elizabeth Sherrill. *Return from Tomorrow*. Grand Rapids, MI: Fleming H. Revell, 1978.

Rogers, Martha E. *An Introduction to the Theoretical Basis of Nursing*. Philadelphia: F.A. Davis, 1970.

Sagan, Samuel. *Entity Possession*. Rochester, VT: Destiny Books, 1994.

Smith, Susy. *The Book of James*. Lincoln, NE: iUniverse.com, Inc., 2000.

Thurman, Robert A. F., translator. *The Tibetan Book of the Dead*. New York: Bantam Books, 1998.

Thurston, Joanie with Wally Johnston. *Possible Fatal*. Portland, OR: Acorn Endeavors, 2004.

Wambach, Helen. *Life Before Life*. New York: Bantam Books, 1979.

———. *Reliving Past Lives*. New York: Bantam Books, 1978.

Whitton, Joel L. and Joe Fisher. *Life Between Life*. New York: Warner Books, 1986.

Wickland, Carl. *Thirty Years Among the Dead*. Van Nuys, CA: Newcastle Publishing Co., 1974.

Williams, Robert M. *Psych-K: The Missing Peace in Your Life!* Crestone, CO: Myrddin, 2004.

About the Author

GARY LEON HILL is an award-winning playwright whose work has been produced at theaters throughout the country. He has received grants from the National Endowment for the Arts, the New York Foundation for the Arts, The Rockefeller Foundation, AT&T, and The Pew Charitable Trusts. His plays include *Food from Trash*, *Back to the Blanket*, *Say Grace*, *In a Beginning*, and *8 Bob Off*. A photographer and filmmaker, Hill worked early in his career with Robert Frank and Rudy Wurlitzer on the films *Life Dances On* and *Energy and How to Get It*. This is his first book. He lives in New York City.